The 10 Symptoms of
Dysfunctional Boards

Your Guide to Great Governance

by Michael J. Steinberg, MA

The 10 Symptoms of Dysfunctional Boards
Your Guide to Great Governance
©2005 Michael J. Steinberg.

I.S.B.N. 0-9770817-0-2

First edition: July 2005

Table of Contents

Appendices

Acknowledgments

I want to express my gratitude to Dave, Kyle, Molly & Bob -- four CEOs who invited me to help them develop their boards, and in the process, showed me four examples of quality leadership. I would also like to express my thanks to Lisa, my partner in business and in life, for her editing, research support and unwavering dedication to this project.

Introduction

This book was written for current board members, potential board members, board chairs and CEOs. For current board members, this book will give you the tools you need to help your board become the best governing body it can be. Potential board members can use this book as a guide to making the best possible contribution to any board they serve, and learn what's in store for them if they choose to take on this very important role. Board chairs are also offered the tools they need to be competent, productive leaders and chairs, and guide their boards to excellence. And it is also a guide to help boards develop themselves into the best and most efficient governing body they can possibly be. For CEOs, this book can help you encourage your boards to serve as a dedicated partner in achieving the vision and goals of the organization.

For philanthropic organizations, this book can help you use the quality of governance in choosing where to commit charitable donations, so that the money donated achieves the greatest amount of good and promotes the ultimate success of the organization. Individuals wishing to make a sizable donation to any organization also need to look for a well-functioning board, and this book can help them as well. A well-functioning board is a sure sign of a well-functioning organization. People who are in a

1

position to make a substantial charitable donation want to know that their gift will be well spent, and will honorably serve the purpose for which it was originally intended. In an effort to do this, smart donors should seek out non-profit organizations run by highly effective, quality boards. Those who look for an apparently well-run organization *first*, and assume there must be a highly functioning board behind it, can end up disappointed if their donation is mismanaged.

Smart donors considering making a major gift to a non-profit organization need to know (for example), who is on the board. Talk with a few of them. Get information from them about their work on the board -- the vision and mission of the organization -- rather than relying on the information provided by fundraisers. I would absolutely work through the board. Too many people give money based on what they *think* an organization is doing, or what it stands for, instead of consciously supporting and investing in a clearly well run organization. That's a big mistake. If I am ready to make a sizable donation, I want to be sure I'm giving it to an organization that's going to use it to advance a noble cause and improve the lives of the people they serve. Wasting a gift is, at the very least, foolish; but blatant mismanagement of donations is a crime!

While I have based this book on 20 years of work with non-profit and public boards, leaders and board members across North America, for-profit organizations can benefit from this information as well. One need only look at the recent headlines to know that many for-profit boards need to clean up their act as well, and a majority of the principles I present are the same.

1

Dysfunctional Boards

Without exception, every board I've every worked with is dysfunctional in some way, and every board member I've ever spoken with can describe at least one dysfunction of their board that causes them intense frustration. Some lament that there are so many problems it's hard to accomplish anything! And yet somehow they plod on. Other board members remain silent, especially new members who are watching the board function for the first time. They may certainly sense a problem, or *feel* some roadblocks to progress, which they may not be able to immediately identify, but they keep quiet. So why don't they speak up? When interviewed, they will often plead inexperience. "Who am I to talk? All these other people have been here for 10 or 15 years!" So they sit there month after month to see if it's just a phase, or a glitch, or a temporary bump in the road. And pretty soon they become acclimated to the existing board culture. They actually stop seeing the dysfunction, and are swept into it.

We have to shake up the world of governance today. **Corruption in corporations is rampant!** The "good old days" where boards could just be "a nice group of volunteers" are gone! The gravity of their role, and the impact on their organizations is greater than it has ever been. Boards across the country are making terrible, costly decisions with very little planning, stealing thousands of hours donated by bright, dedicated people, wasting them in meaningless meetings, and mis-spending millions of charitable dollars. This is not acceptable. Non-profit boards are in crisis... but there is hope!

In our society today, there is an increasing need for charitable work -- a need to help people who cannot help themselves. And so many of these services are primarily provided by non-profit organizations. In order for them to meet this enormous challenge, we **must** have boards that are savvy, boards comprised of bright people, dedicated to learning and growing within their roles. Board members today must know their jobs and be willing to make tough decisions.

In the past, all we needed were volunteers, nice, well-meaning, wonderful people, directed by the administrator or the executive of the organization, and willing to do whatever they were told. **Those days are gone.** No matter where you live, in every part of the country, from coast to coast, there are far greater expectations and responsibilities attached to being a member of a board of directors. The quality of life for millions of people is at stake, and it's time for boards to meet the critical new challenges of great governance today. It's time to be smart, get active and stay dedicated.

Next to being a parent, there are very few jobs in our society where we are given so much responsibility over the very *lives* of other people, with little or no training required. Every day parents make decisions that affect the lives of their children. And meanwhile, across the country, board members are making decisions that affect the lives of millions -- not only those directly served by their organization, but family members, employees and everyone in the community. Far too often, those decisions are made in misguided, highly dysfunctional ways!

Dysfunctional boards are not inept or incompetent by *intent*, but by virtue of the simple fact that nobody took the time to *train* them. And all too often, boards feel guilty about investing organizational funds into training and developing their own skills as board members. Guilt, be gone. People are not born with the necessary skills to be productive board members, nor are those skills acquired magically at some moment in time, shortly before a person's first board meeting! Training and developing the board is one of the smartest investments an organization can make.

For a board to neglect themselves is one of the biggest and potentially costliest mistakes they can make. When boards develop into highly functional entities, and become the very best they can be, their planning, decisions and actions can positively affect thousands of lives every day. This is so BIG, but apparently (and surprisingly) not well known. I was amazed years ago when a board member from a rural nursing home in Minnesota approached me after a presentation and remarked, "Wow! I had no idea how important this work is... and I've been on this board for 12 years!"

Depending on the kind of organization you serve, a life could actually hang in the balance of the board decisions you make. It is an awesome responsibility and should be respected as such. If it's a long-term care facility or social service board, the decisions you make may have a tremendous impact on the lives and futures of the people you serve -- AND those who are hired to serve them -- namely the employees. Nobody seems to remember that the livelihood, morale, and ability of employees everywhere to do their jobs well every day is based on board decisions. Using books like this and conducting formal board training is an investment in excellence, organizational success and improving the lives of everyone we serve.

The job of the board has changed and so we must get sophisticated in governance. It's a serious role that must be explained to potential board members *before* they sign on. It's time for board members to realize the importance of what they do, their main functions, and their critical decision-making role on behalf of any organization they serve.

In this complex society, the traditional role of the board -- approving and overseeing the annual budget -- is now just *one* of their responsibilities. Board members can no longer sit back and merely react to changes and crises, but today must actively serve their organizations, working to create and sustain an organizational vision, and foster any changes that are needed to achieve that vision.

Non-Profit Mismanagement

The American Red Cross raised almost a billion dollars, specifically earmarked for the Liberty Disaster Relief Fund following the attacks on the World Trade Center towers in New York City, September 11, 2001. When the Red Cross did not clearly convey to contributors that their money may *not* go to people directly affected by the attacks, or to aid the rescue workers at the attack sites, the public outcry prompted a hostile House Subcommittee to question the American Red Cross' CEO. The CEO resigned over differences with the organization's board about how to spend the money in the Liberty Fund. Not only were donors angry and concerned, but the mismanagement of *information* about how the money was to be spent caused a wave of mistrust about where all kinds of charitable dollars were actually going, and other charities were hurt in the fallout.

The United Way, another highly respected icon in the world of non-profit, charitable organizations, has also found its way into the headlines a number of times over the past decade -- once when the national president was convicted of fraud for misusing the organization's assets. But where was the board? Who was serving as the guardian over the $3 billion United Way received each year in donations? It was not the board who was holding the president accountable, but pressure from representatives of the 14 largest United Ways that put the focus on the President and actions that should be taken to repair the damage that had been done. That is the job of the board. And when the board is not on the job, the financial consequences can be far-reaching and devastating. And when they hit the headlines again a few years ago, with the former CEO of United Way in the D.C. area pleading guilty to defrauding the charity of nearly half a million dollars, public trust was damaged, and this time, the entire board was replaced!

By 2003, the National Committee for Responsive Philanthropy reported that workplace giving programs offering *alternatives to United Way campaigns* had grown almost 36% between 1996-2001. Individual donors are speaking volumes with their wallets, and United Way has been forced to shift their entire fundraising focus.

And now Congress is getting involved. A 2005 bill is being introduced to crack down on the nations 1.3 million nonprofit groups if they don't do a better job of regulating themselves. Independent Sector, an umbrella group of the nation's largest charities and foundations, issued a report encouraging nonprofits to adopt conflict of interest policies, ensure boards have members with financial skills and, among other things, get an independent audit of their finances.

Crisis of Confidence

A 2002 survey of over 1,000 adults, conducted by the Barna Research Group, found that 23% -- almost one quarter of respondents -- said they had lost confidence in nonprofits, with the *least* confident falling in the donor age group of 57-75 (traditionally the most generous demographic).

They reported that 58% of donors dropped their financial support of a nonprofit because they felt the organization was no longer trustworthy or reliable. Outstanding boards and great governance are no longer an option. All eyes are on you now.

You may find my expose of the flaws I've seen in boards throughout the years, and criticism of their actions, might be irritating and uncomfortable reading, especially for existing board members who may be experiencing some similar dysfunctions in their own boards. The discomfort you're feeling is intentional. I may be irritating in the beginning, but hopefully, by the end of this book, you will learn ways to solve each of the dysfunctions I'll be outlining, so that, like an oyster dealing with an irritating grain of sand, you will be able to systematically and diligently attend to yourself as a board, until you've created a pearl! My role is to serve as a catalyst to quality and success in the world of non-profit governance.

2

Overview

Understanding the Role

The first major cause of dysfunctional boards is people not understanding the gravity of the role to begin with. People begin their terms on a board truly dedicated to the organization and/or what it stands for, but often think it's their job to rubber-stamp the requests of the administration. That's all they are there for, and many times (particularly on larger boards) they don't even show up for meetings! As boards get bigger and bigger, and people feel less and less important, it becomes easy not to attend meetings. How could you be missed? I can't tell you the number of boards that are totally puzzled when I utter the immortal words, "Mandatory attendance." They may say it's not fair to require that of a "volunteer." They may suggest that it can't be done -- it can't be enforced. And I say that not only *can* you demand it, you **must**! When board members don't show up, they are shirking a serious responsibility. I know this is irritating, but remember your goal -- to create a pearl.

Unless there's a dire family event (and there better be only <u>one</u> of those in a year), there's no excuse for missing or skipping a board meeting. The concept of building a bigger board just to be sure enough people will show up, is a farce... and it's risky.

At a board workshop I conducted on the East Coast, I asked how many people, out of a 90-member board, generally show up for meetings. I ventured, "20?" And someone chuckled, "If that!" One of the first problems with that is -- are they the same 20?

Every board member is a member of a *unified* body, and **legally** bound by the decisions made by whoever shows up. And mark my words, some day a board is going to make a decision that yields catastrophic consequences, and the courts and the legal system will hold ALL 90 board members liable for the decision that was made by that small quorum of the board.

When you consider joining a board, take it seriously, or don't get involved. When nominating or choosing board members, search for people who are truly going to BE there. Don't just select people because they're wealthy, famous, or as an extension of a friendship. Board members should be chosen for their involvement, willingness to grow and change, and for their ability to be active learners. I have met many members of boards who seriously have no business being there. Organizations, especially non-profits, cannot afford rabble-rousers or those who join to advance their own personal agendas, at the expense of the people who are supposed to be served by the organization.

In this economy, and with ever-diminishing governmental support, charitable organizations must be more responsible than ever before. Being a board member today is serious business, but potentially a great source of pride. This is a volunteer contribution people can make toward creating a better world, and this book is designed to fully support and encourage boards to do the best possible job, and become the most skilled and successful board the organization has ever seen.

To Serve, or Not to Serve...

After 20 years of working with boards, and conducting thousands of interviews throughout the U.S. and Canada, my research shows that the number one reason people join boards is because someone simply asked them. And like the voice in the movie "Field of Dreams" which implores, "Build it and they will come," so too it seems board members are just out there waiting -- ask them, and they will serve.

That's powerful when you think about it. But when you ask someone to serve on a board, it is critical today to honestly represent board membership as a responsibility -- an honor, often a joy, but the bottom line is, that it's a, sometimes awesome, responsibility.

I have also discovered through the years, that the number one reason board members **quit** is because they feel their time was wasted. The biggest problem with a board that is dysfunctional, is that you may get good people, who are truly willing to dedicate their time and energy, but their time is often wasted by the things you do (or don't do) as a board. Then these very valuable people leave, and the ones who stay may very well be problematic. They'll stay for personal gain, rather than for the benefit of the organization.

Each of the 10 symptoms I will outline relates to time wasting. When a board is dysfunctional, it even *feels* like a waste of time to the people serving on it. They feel their input doesn't matter, and may question why they're even on the board. They can feel that their time is actually being misused. Board members are busy people and that must be respected and appreciated. Some of them may be on a number of other boards. They come to meetings run by people who are inept at meeting management, with agendas that are a mess, and with board chairs who love to pontificate and waste time. Trust me. It's rampant. All of these issues will be addressed in the coming chapters. Big boards -- gigantic boards also waste time with too much interaction, too much information that needs to be shared, and just too many people. After I describe the 10 Symptoms of Dysfunctional Boards, people who are on a board, or interact with one, will be able to "score" their board in each of the areas outlined.

This book will describe the main dysfunctions, their causes and their solutions, to help boards create an environment where the job gets done, board members feel a strong sense of satisfaction in what they do, and the organization and the people they serve are helped in the best possible ways.

Leadership - Collaboration - Mentoring

Before the new millennium rolled over, I was asked to do a presentation on what I thought the future was going to hold for us. Because of my work developing corporate leaders, organizational leaders and governance leadership, three themes came to me: Leadership, Collaboration and Mentoring. We must continue to improve our leadership skills at all levels. We must see the importance of and become excellent at collaborating with those around us. And we must realize that mentoring others to be successful will have a profound impact on the success of all of us in the future.

To say that we must continue to improve our **leadership** skills at all levels, I mean that we have to consider all the new technologies of leadership, and incorporate the best from everything that's available, in order to improve our own personal leadership skills. We have to understand what works and what doesn't work, more than we ever have before. That's just the first step. Even great leadership cannot stand alone in the successful future of today's organizations.

We have to become truly skilled at collaborating, and put it on a more conscious level. We need outstanding **collaboration** between board members, between the board and management, and between the board and the community. It is a litmus test for organizational success in the future. "Collaborate" is a fascinating word because it has seemingly contradictory definitions. In the dictionary, to collaborate is "to work together," but it also means "to cooperate with an enemy!" In our world filled with diverse ideas and values, what often starts out feeling like we're cooperating with the enemy ends up creating a collegial, partnering relationship and turns into a process for working more collaboratively together. Collaboration is assertively reaching out to individuals and organizations in an attempt to develop colleagues. Embracing something that may be foreign to you, or something you wouldn't normally connect with, is critical to creating effective collaborations, necessary for success in the future.

When people think of collaboration, we think of teamwork, cooperating and joint ventures. But there's another type of collaboration -- a collaboration of ideas and philosophies that at first glance appear to be opposing forces. One powerful example that I regularly experience in my work, is the collaboration between business and financial success, versus spirituality and maintaining high ethical practices. But a collaboration CAN be created without compromising either entity.

There is a Fortune 500 company, a highly profitable energy giant, that is being essentially run by the CEO and a former monk. Their working relationship is based on "doing the right thing" and they describe it as the story of "two unusual and dedicated humanists who are able to keep their focus on profits and ethics at the same time." The monk, who had left the church and was working in the human resources department, became known for his logic and personnel knowledge. The CEO eventually sought out the monk's wisdom for more and more of the "people" issues in the organization, and because of his success, the monk eventually began to report directly to the CEO. Every decision the company makes has an ethical base to it, and after 10 years of working together, the two are inseparable and the company has grown from a small, local utility monopoly, into one of the nation's largest and fastest-growing energy providers. They even wrote a book about their collaboration, called "The CEO and the Monk: One Company's Journey to Profit and Purpose" (by Catell, Moore & Rifkin, John Wiley & Sons Canada, Ltd. ©2004).

For faith-based organizations of any denomination, if there is a positive, spiritual, humanistic and values-based foundation to everything you do, the organization is going to be a better place (as long as you don't get rigid about it). It's developing the proper blend of business and ethical elements that will lead you in a more positive and prosperous direction.

One CEO I worked with extensively was responsible for a large number of long-term care facilities. Some were affiliated with an organized religious group, and some were non-denominational. He was an expert at the business side of long-term care, but also made sure the organization didn't lose sight of its spiritual side. He attributed his success to that balance, and the ultimate long-range success of any organization may well depend on achieving that same kind of balance.

When I say "spiritual," I am not necessarily talking about the involvement of any organized religion. Ethical guidelines do not have to be religiously based. The spiritual sense that boards need is more of a core belief that there is a greater responsibility we must acknowledge when we make decisions affecting human beings. That's why I like spiritually-based organizations, because they see themselves responding to a higher calling, doing work for a greater good. And I prefer mission statements with a ethical, yet non-denominational element to them. It's important to accept everyone. It has to be there, and it has to emanate from the top. Believe me, there was no moral compass guiding the Enron board of directors or senior management. Enron was, in fact, described in one publication as "a *culture* of impropriety." And similarly, in the story of the Tyco debacle, as one board member put it, "There was corruption, collusion and concealment at the very top levels of management, which made it very hard for the outside directors to detect." Once again, what was missing, was any semblance of a "moral compass" guiding the organization from the very top. All it takes is a little sense of spirit and higher calling to influence every organizational decision in a healthy, helpful and ethical way.

The ethical foundation aids the organization's ability to collaborate in other, more traditional ways as well. Beyond the organization's outreach to the community, *internal* collaboration must be tuned. Boards need to see themselves in a collaborative role with their CEO, and CEOs have to stop seeing themselves as separate from, or positioned in any kind of adversarial role to their boards. The CEO and the board are a team.

In analyzing success in the new millennium, the third critical theme is the importance of **mentoring**. We must actively and consciously *help* people be successful. In a technologically-advanced society, we no longer have the time to let people learn through the "school of hard knocks." This applies to boards as well. New board members are brought in with a hearty handshake and a warm, "Welcome!" and then often find themselves rather isolated. There is generally no one helping them become skilled at what they need to do. Just like everyone who came before them, new board members are expected to learn the hard way. We must stop that, NOW. It is time that we make it an **obligation** for every board member to mentor at least one new board member.

In the organization itself, experience is also critical. Mentoring diminishes the hierarchy and caste systems so prevalent today. It creates a more collaborative environment. Bosses don't see themselves as "better than" their employees. People need to feel included. They need to feel they belong, that they matter and that they're an important part of the whole organizational picture. That's what mentoring and collaboration are all about. From a pragmatic standpoint, the need for competent, rapid decision-making is so significant today, we can no longer afford the time to wait for people to learn on their own, whether they are board members, or employees of the organization.

In this new millennium, we must focus on becoming more skilled leaders, educated in the latest theories and practices of effective leadership. Thoughtful, intentional collaboration must be incorporated, and along with that, a program of conscious, respectful mentoring. With those three keys, you can expect success at all levels -- from governance and organizational leadership, through the entire organization, and filtering out into the community you serve.

3

The Challenge of Change

Everything is changing! The world is changing. Anybody disagree? It's more complex. Technology is changing and improving on a daily basis, and people's values about what is important are changing faster than ever before. For the first time in history, our working adult society includes people in *four* different generational groups, each group functioning with its own set of values. "Generations at Work: Managing the Clash of Veterans, Boomers, Xers and Nexters in Your Workplace" (by Zemke, Raines & Filipczak, AMACOM Publishing ©2000) does an outstanding job of deciphering the values differences from generation to generation, helping people understand, respect and work more effectively with each other.

The world is more complex, and the economy more global. We live in an increasingly international society now, so the values of other cultures affect our work world more than ever before. In neighborhoods across America the diversity of our communities is growing faster than ever in history. We can't stop change -- we're IN it! So we have to educate ourselves about change. And one of the main purposes of a board, any board, is to deal with change.

Change isn't as simple as it may seem. It is a complex concept that comes in three distinct (and sometimes piggybacking) types -- Sudden Change, Anticipated Change and Fostered Change. And what I've discovered is that when you understand the three different *types* of change, dealing with change becomes more clear, more natural, easier to do, and substantially less stressful!

Sudden Change

The type of change we're most familiar with is Sudden Change. It just happens. You don't know it's coming. All of a sudden there's a problem at work and you have to adjust. You had no clue a person or event or a system was going to change, but it did. We humans are very good at sudden change. And for many of us, it can be exciting. It *tests* us and we love to rise to the challenge and respond quickly. It's an adrenaline rush. We spend a lot of our lives learning how to respond to sudden change.

Boards, on the other hand, cannot be just involved in sudden change, nor can leaders. Even though it can be exciting and we're good at it; and even if it's something we're experienced at dealing with, a life of reaction does not build a successful future for any organization. We have to start thinking about the other two types of change.

Anticipated Change

Anticipated Change is predictable and something we can prepare for. And today, for the first time in human history, we can think about, visualize and more accurately "anticipate" change through computer modeling and advancements in technology. We can enlist the wisdom of futurists and utilize trend data. There are all kinds of methods to help us see change coming, and yet I am amazed at how few organizations truly *anticipate* change at the level they should.

I still deal with boards that don't do long-range planning very efficiently (if at all). Long-range planning *is* anticipating change. In a highly volatile and competitive society, long-range planning is essential to the success of an organization. Whether you're doing three-year, 5-year, or 10-year planning, it's fine, but you have to do it.

National organizations are doing a lot more now, looking at modeling, statistical projections and futuring. It's exciting and wonderful. Boards need to spend a greater amount of their time *anticipating* change and helping the organization *prepare* for change. This is especially true in the work I've done in long-term care. We have trends that were identified years ago, that we're still not adequately responding to. This whole new world of assisted living isn't just suddenly starting to accelerate. We've known about it for a *very* long time.

We don't really *like* anticipating change. Why else would 30 million people wait to turn in their taxes on the last possible day? (And 10 million more turn them in months late!) But we're not alone. Over half the taxpayers in Taiwan also failed to file until the last two days. So while it's sort of a universal trait, there's still something wrong here. And that's the point. For the dawdling taxpayer, waiting until that last moment makes the issue sudden and urgent and a bit exciting! (When in fact it was totally anticipated all along). We do this kind of thing all the time. But **not** anticipating change is a human trait that organizations cannot afford any longer. Organizations and boards must get serious and consciously anticipate change.

Fostered Change

The third type of change, Fostered Change, is more important than it's ever been, and the kind of change people spend the *least* amount of time on. Fostered Change is change that we actually **create**. We make it happen. We say to ourselves or our organizations, "Okay, we need to create a better workplace -- a place where people want to come and give their best." This is change we **choose** in order to make our organizations more viable and successful.

Fostered Change should be a big part of long-range planning. Fostering change prepares you. And if it's done well, with true vision, it incorporates changes you may be anticipating, and can even reduce the need to react to a sudden change. When you focus on fostering change in your organization, you consciously look for things that are coming, and are less often surprised or caught "off guard."

Boards I've worked with spend little, if any time on fostered change, unless it's a derivative of long-range planning (so it happens by accident). I think boards and leaders of organizations should actually call for a "fostered change" meeting, where they decide exactly what they need to change to make the organization better and more successful. Fostering comes from the top.

When we "foster" anything, the goal is to motivate it and move it. It's gentle, steady and purposeful. So why is it done so seldom? In my experience, I've seen a lot of what I call the "John Wayne Syndrome" happening in this country. The characters played by John Wayne were all masters of sudden change. Everything changed suddenly and he'd react! He'd strap on his guns, go out, and deal with the problem. It would be a very boring movie if John Wayne sat there and said, "You know, if I plan ahead and strategize, I don't think the bad guys will come after us." No. It wouldn't make an exciting movie.

I remember working with an executive about 20 years ago, and we were looking at long-range planning ideas. At one point, the executive said "Well, I really don't want to plan *too* much." "Why?" I asked. "Because then life would be boring!" That's our culture. We still want excitement, even in the workplace.

It's that excitement -- the "rush" we get from dealing with sudden change that makes it hard for us to think about a situation where we are so prepared that the change doesn't present a big enough challenge for us when it happens. Please, if you want excitement, go to the movies, rather than putting your organization into a panic every now and then for your own thrill.

Now the movie analogy is fun and simple, but there are some life or death examples that may bring this important concept out a little more poignantly. There was an earthquake that hit Armenia in 1988, killing 25,000 people. The earthquake was a "sudden" change for them. There was little or no time to react before thousands perished.

Just one year later, another earthquake measuring a bit *higher* on the Richter Scale, hit San Francisco, and 67 people died. But in San Francisco, earthquakes are *anticipated*. It is just assumed that they will happen again. For California, it's a science, and seismologists are constantly working on anticipating the next quake with the greatest possible precision. They are even experimenting with explosives to make small adjustments on potentially volatile fault lines, in an effort to prevent a major quake. Architects and engineers are also continually improving structural design to make buildings more resistant to damage from inevitable -- "anticipated" -- earthquakes.

It was anticipating change and preparing for it that greatly minimized the loss of life in San Francisco.

In the aftermath of the recent catastrophic tsunami in Indonesia, scientists across the globe are banding together to create a way to gauge seismic changes on the ocean floor. Their goal is to be able to anticipate future events of this kind, and prevent the kind of horrific consequences and incredible loss of life that occurred at the end of 2004.

Boards have to change their "reactionary" mentality, and CEOs must keep their boards informed. Boards have to get involved in fostering change for the future. The board must actively take on that task. Boards are not created to serve executives as a "yes" group, a rubber stamp for everything the CEO thinks the organization needs to do. That is NOT the job of the board. The board needs to be actively, consciously involved in defining and fostering the future of the organization, in a collaborative partnership with the CEO.

I've seen a lot of long-range plans come from management. Management decides they need a plan, presents their ideas to the board, and the board approves the plan. WRONG! It should be a team effort. The board should be equally involved with management in long-range planning.

The board should also be involved with the executive in evolving the **mission** of the organization. The executive is a big part of it, and I see no problem with the CEO making suggestions, but when all is said and done, the board really has to "own" the mission. They must "buy" into it, believe it, foster it, and ultimately fund it!

The key to looking at this idea of fostered change and anticipated change is to ask what the next five or 10 years are going to bring to your industry. For non-profit and charitable organizations, I believe the upcoming leadership challenges will include the following:

1. Fundraising. This has become such a big issue for so many organizations that they spend most of their time worrying and talking about it, and don't spend enough time on the *other* areas boards need to be addressing. Too much focus on fundraising puts the board and the organization off balance and detracts from their success. They have to get better at fundraising -- whether they use consultants, create their own fundraising programs, or use other techniques. The most important issue is that it must be better conceptualized. As a board, they must also look at what their fundraising role is. This topic is discussed in more detail later in the book.

2. Dealing with Change Itself. Boards have to look at their role in helping the organization make changes that, while not required, will ultimately make them a better organization. Continuous quality improvement, and construction upgrades are all a part of fostered change. The purpose of leadership is to foster positive change. Fostered change keeps an organization vital, creating a better future and helping the organization survive longer and stronger in the marketplace. Change is now a part of everyday success, and organizations have to teach people to handle change better. They have to make change "work" for people.

3. Improving the workplace. This is a significant challenge, especially for service organizations. We have to make a commitment to making the workplace a highly functioning, rewarding place to be for 40 (or more) hours a week. Effective service to customers, clients and co-workers is directly affected by the quality of the work environment. When you create a work environment that is positive, respectful and encouraging, the impact of that is directly reflected in the way service providers treat their customers. Non-existent and/or poor customer service is often a reflection of a work environment that is less than desirable.

Improving the workplace IS the board's responsibility because it has to be conceptualized, funded, *and* management has to be given the tools to do it. Management must also be carefully selected for their ability to make sure they can create and maintain a quality workplace. If the board doesn't put it on the front burner, it won't happen. It's so often the *last* thing people do. Believe me, I know this. Throughout my career, I have been called in to help clients resolve severe workplace issues that could have been avoided by a more proactive approach.

You know it too. The courts today are filled with "hostile work environment" and harassment lawsuits. The EEOC (Equal Employment Opportunity Commission) reported that over 20,000 complaints alleging employment discrimination were filed with them in 2003. The average jury award to employees in sexual harassment suits, is $250,000 plus attorney fees and litigation costs.

Organizations need "fostered change" plans to make it a better place to work -- a place where people collaborate and care about each other, treat each other respectfully and where there are methods for determining the people who work well together and helping those who don't. Addressing policies related to employee satisfaction and morale may not be the most enjoyable work for a board. What boards *really* like is the physical stuff, the new properties, the buildings, the land, the things they can point to and say, "We built that." It's much more gratifying than saying, "We made people happier. We made employees love to work here." Most would rather leave those areas up to management. But this is important! Creating the vision and values of a quality workplace and developing quality workplace policies must be on the agenda of every board, and sufficient money and resources must be allocated to make it happen.

I have learned over the years that large groups tend to have what I call "group inertia." Very often, it takes a shake-up to get a group of people to realize they need to change -- they need to look at what they can do to be different and, by virtue of that, better. Remember my job as that grain of sand in the oyster? Well, I'm here to irritate you and challenge you. Dr. Phil McGraw puts it squarely, "Is it workin' for you?" As a board you have to stay on your toes and keep asking yourself if you are getting the most out of the very important, very dedicated people who work for your organization -- who come here every day to make this organization what it needs to be. And are you giving them the most? Have you created an inspiring mission and clear values worthy of following? And from that line of questioning, I hope I can be a catalyst toward creating your pearl, no matter what your position in the organization, or your role in its success.

Unbridled Power

I can't play my role without shaking you up. And throughout my workshops, and in boardrooms across the country, some people may feel irritated, but ultimately challenged to make things better. Think of your power to improve peoples lives in the world. Non-profit boards have immense power to positively influence the lives of millions of people across this country (maybe second only after the power of government). This is a serious, awesome power that must be considered, respected, and used responsibly.

Board power is unbridled power -- phenomenal power over whatever it chooses. The key to success in boards is very similar to what Chrysler did years ago when they made major changes in their corporation and in their products. The slogan "We Questioned Everything" described a new philosophy where the leadership of the organization questioned the bedrock of what they were doing. Armed with that mandate, Chrysler design engineers came up with some of the most innovative car concepts ever. To this day, car companies are still copying the "cab-forward" innovation and some of the other ideas that came out of "questioning everything." Don't hold anything in your organizations sacred, until you've looked at it. Then, rekindle the sacred things that are *worth* rekindling and make the powerful, positive changes that you, as a board, need to make.

Bygone Bylaws

When's the last time you looked at your **bylaws**? (Are you feeling the irritation of the sand in your shell, just reading that word?) Bylaws are more important than you realize. Boards don't really worry about them -- often try to avoid addressing them -- and yet the board is *bound* by them! There are an awful lot of what I call "Bygone Bylaws" out there, antiquated, boilerplate bylaws that don't meet the needs of the organizations they're written for! Outmoded missions are also rampant. Revisit your mission to be sure it speaks to what the organization really stands for. Look at it. Think about it and rework it until it says what you *really* want it to say.

The missions of some spiritually-based organizations, written some time ago, may no longer accurately or properly address the broader, more egalitarian populations they are currently serving. The big issue is, do they want or *need* to change the mission to reflect changes in the organization, or not? If they don't, fine. Not too long ago I worked with a religious order that consciously decided to remain as a service exclusively for nuns and retired nuns. They had every right to limit their mission and make that choice. But it's something that should be examined.

Why do boards today have to change? Particularly for non-profit boards, change is just going to happen to you, and you're going to be left floundering and choking in the dust if you don't seize the moment, look hard at what's coming down the road, and make the very most of it. Some of the central issues these boards are going to have to deal with in the near future include:

1. Decreasing availability of public funds
2. Increasing competition for private funds
3. A shift in the values, expectations and diversity of the population
4. Increasing diversity in the spectrum of services
5. Increasing competition or competitive forces
6. Increasing scrutiny from the public and government in all services
7. Changing technology and lengthening life span. A longer life span affects a lot of services.

4

The Changing Roles of a Board

Now before we can talk about the dysfunctional aspects of boards, I think it's important to begin with the question of why boards exist in the first place. What are their main roles? It is different today, so we have to look at boards in a new way.

Traditionally, the purpose of a board was to serve as an organization's financial watchdog. And governance was really viewed as stewardship, making sure that the financial, physical, and even the human resources were prudently used for the sake of the organization.

When I first started working with boards 20 years ago, most of the organizations I dealt with didn't have a formal, stated mission. Missions were more likely assumed. If an organization *did* have a mission, it came from an affiliated group of some kind, like a church that was part of the organization, and they just used the church's mission. It wasn't even a mission such as we know them today, and very few organizations had anything beyond that. Nobody had a "vision" statement of where they wanted to be in the future. The purpose of a board, was to make sure the organization was true to the bottom line and their organizational purpose (more or less). Today, that is absolutely NOT enough!

Visionary - Guardian - Link

To remain a simple, old-fashioned "watchdog" board will ultimately render the organization useless. For boards today, this is the most critical issue. In today's changing, moving, demanding and *litigious* world, boards must now serve three distinct, major roles, all equal in value: They must serve as a **visionary**, as a **guardian** and equally as a **link**. And a board can be good at all three, but the bigger issue is that they must see the *importance* of all three roles.

Visionary

Visionary is the role of futuring -- of making sure the organization is successful in the months and years ahead. As organizational visionaries, board members actually help define the future, and create the resource paths and capabilities to achieve that future. Board time must be consciously devoted to thinking about the future, and getting the information necessary to know what's coming up technologically, governmentally or socially for the business, industry or service your organization provides. In other words, you must anticipate and foster change. Armed with facts about your industry, trends and predictions, you must see the future as best you can, define your organization's place in that future, and make sure you have a CEO who can actively guide the organization to a successful place in that future. These are the challenges and the responsibilities that come with the visionary role.

It is essential that the board be part of this process. In too many organizations, seeing the future and finding your most successful path into it, is a job left for the CEO to do, and for the board to merely endorse. But that's not fulfilling the board's visionary role!

As true visionaries, the board creates the organization's purpose, mission and guiding values. They keep the organization focused on its future and strategic opportunities.

Strategic planning is also part of the visionary role. Any future decision-making needs to be gauged against a board-created set of guiding principles and values. They become the compass by which the organization is steered into the future. Creating (or re-creating) the mission, vision and values statements are also all part of this. The goal is to make sure the organization has a successful, defined future.

One board I worked with decided they were going to have "visioning" meetings, set up quarterly. For a couple hours each quarter, a meeting was specifically devoted to visioning. Another board decided to actually create a Visioning Committee, which is also an excellent idea.

Guardian

The second, and equally important role for a board member, is the role of **guardian**. Boards have been doing this forever, but let me expand the definition of it for you. This is the more traditional role, protecting the organization's resources, organizational values and their heritage. It also includes the responsibilities of providing the policies, board-level decisions, and resources necessary to insure the organization stays financially sound and lives up to its mission.

But another important piece that I work with boards on is defining the "cultural assets" of their organizations. Boards need to examine what makes the organization unique, special and valuable. Some answers may take you back in history. Some may take you back to the question of why the organization was founded and how it all began. That relates to heritage. Some organizations in this country are over 100 years old, and boards need to understand why they've lasted that long. Boards that appreciate the rich heritage of the organization, will do a better job as guardians, and will want to cherish and preserve the very best of an organization's history and reputation. This is a part of the true role of the board member as an organizational guardian.

Every board needs to have this powerful discussion. They need to define, in writing, what the organization is, what their true

29

purpose is, and what they believe. In a sense, they need to define the organization's personality, and why they're so great!

As guardians, board members also need to know what physical resources the organization has, and what their infrastructure is. Those must be maintained as well.

There are some organizations -- some hospitals for example -- that started with a group of people who wanted to provide affordable healthcare to the poor. Those are heritage pieces, those are "guardian" pieces. Board members must also serve as guardians of the organization's *human* resources, holding leaders accountable for creating a work environment that makes employees and volunteers feel fostered, mentored and devoted, and helps everyone feel they're working for a great organization!

Some organizations are highly skilled at providing specialized services for people. The Mayo Clinic in Minnesota is a good example of that. To be considered a world-class medical establishment becomes an actual part of their heritage and their board becomes the guardian of the organization's reputation, and the skills and unique capabilities of the people who provide those services. The board is responsible for maintaining the organization's status in their industry, and in the world.

Guardians watch over more than money and facilities. They guard the well-being of the people and the organization's heritage as well.

At this point I think it's important to talk a little bit about the importance of striking a balance between the roles of visionary and guardian. As a visionary, you put your focus on the future and the changes that will be needed to keep the organization vital and successful. As the guardian, the focus is on the present and the past, identifying and preserving the best of what the organization has to offer. To make changes, just for the sake of making changes, under the auspices of serving as an organizational "visionary," can actually harm the organization. Changes that discard the valuable qualities of the organizational culture, or disregard the value of long-term employees, can ultimately hurt the function and the reputation of the organization. For vision to be truly valuable, and for change to truly *enhance* the organization, what must be taken into consideration are all the things that work (remember, if it ain't broke...), what is valuable, and what is historically sound. This is a powerful balance that must be struck, between being a visionary and serving as a guardian for the essence and the best of the organization.

Link

Equally important with those two, is the third role -- the necessity for board members to serve as a positive **link** connecting the organization, the community and the people they serve. This is the organization's connection with the major stakeholders and financial supporters. Part of a board member's role is to stay positively connected to the community, informed, involved and active.

A board that is well chosen to begin with, will be a representation of the communities around it. Fulfilling the role as a link requires that your board members feel proud to serve, and are eager to discuss with others their affiliation with the organization. Board members who are effectively serving as a link, are also constantly looking for new board members -- people who will serve the board well, exhibit outstanding leadership skills, or who have skills in other areas that will serve the organization. Board members who are great links also have a knowledge of the local press and understand the press' relationship and history with the organization. These are board members who know the demographics of the community, and have a sense of how the community views the organization. Yes! This is a lot of responsibility, but being a link can also be exciting and fun!

As a board member, it's not solely up to you to procure all the knowledge you need. Part of this responsibility falls on the shoulders of management. The organization's leadership will have experts in some of these areas. For example, the Director of Public Relations (PR) can help the board understand the organization's relationship with the press. Specific staff members are often brought in to help educate the board. The executive cannot possibly be an expert on everything! It's the CFO who has the wealth of financial knowledge, and the HR Director who has the human resource expertise, etc. Not only can the board gain a wealth of knowledge from these internal experts, but it also affords board members a first-hand look at the richness of talent that is managing the organization on a day-to-day basis.

5

Dysfunction Junction

In my work with boards throughout the U.S. and Canada, I have had occasion to work with large groups representing CEOs, chairs and members from many boards. Through my interactions with them, I've gained a lot of information. I've also worked with many individual boards and part of my process, is to conduct personal interviews with a representative group of board members, learn what their real issues are, and determine what is getting in the way of their ability to feel good about their involvement with the board.

Through my research and the wealth of information I have gained from these board members, I have defined 10 common symptoms -- 10 major categories of dysfunction in non-profit boards today. Arguably, there are more than these, but I'll leave that up to you. And while it's important to point out that this research comes from non-profit boards, based on what's going on in boardrooms across this country, there are enough similarities in for-profit companies, to make this book helpful to all of them. I believe every board has some problems, and I encourage you to rate your own board as you go through the book.

It is only when you have a sense of where you think your board **is**, that you can truly be a catalyst toward making things better, improving your organization, and moving them away from Dysfunction Junction. Your board may have just a few areas to work on, while some boards need help in every category! The key is to try to repair the dysfunctions and move forward, creating a board that works positively and productively for the organization and all the people you serve.

We **owe** it to the people we serve. We **owe** it to the employees. And if your purpose is not to make it a better board and help the organization, then you owe it to the organization to excuse yourself, or choose not to be involved from the start. It is **not enough** to show up to meetings, or have your name printed on the letterhead. Being a board member today is a commitment to continual involvement in making that board the best it can be, and helping the organization be the best it can be. Dealing with the symptoms of dysfunction will have a lasting, positive, healthy effect on the organization.

Consider this book a "wellness program" for your board. Boards must dedicate time and money to maximizing the impact of their involvement with the organization. And they have to do it in a way that creates a legacy of ongoing improvement for every new board member who signs on. What very often happens, is that the board generates some improvement, but doesn't make the effort to write it down, or **create policy**. Then, as the board leadership evolves, previous improvements can shift, be discarded, or become completely forgotten, and it's back to the old ways.

The 10 Symptoms of Dysfunctional Boards

To prevent the problems that come with a board that is not working at optimal level, the first step is to recognize the symptoms of dysfunctional boards:

1. Foggy Focus
2. Dollar $ign Delusion
3. Bigger-is-Better Fixation
4. Dysfunctional Diversity
5. Turnstile Leadership
6. Altruistic Self-Interest
7. Jurisdictional Jungle
8. Misguided Meetings
9. Decision Paralysis
10. Minutia Mania

"Dys" Way to the Boardroom

Every board has issues. Every board has dysfunctions. Just like people -- nobody's perfect. As a diagnostic tool, this book can help you see what the **key** symptoms are and identify which one(s) apply to your board. It can help you understand how and why they happen, and help board members and leaders determine what changes can be made to improve the board, and ultimately the organization. If you're new to a board and see any of the main symptoms outlined, you can use the book to support your problem-solving ideas so that you can act as a catalyst to change -- to create the pearl within your board and make it better.

For those of you who are currently serving on a board, there is a place at the end of the book (Appendix I), where you can actually rate your board on each of the 10 Symptoms. Before you move to the next symptom, stop, reflect for a moment, and give your board a rating of 1-5 -- with a 1 representing little or no problems in this area, and a score of 5 representing a severe level of dysfunction, in your opinion.

6

Foggy Focus

To paraphrase a famous line from Lewis Carroll's book "Alice's Adventures in Wonderland," "If you don't know where you're going, then it doesn't matter which way you go." And the key to recognizing Foggy Focus as a possible dysfunction of your board, is if you perceive no clear sense of direction at many levels.

Foggy Mission, Vision & Values

Boards with a Foggy Focus suffer from unclear mission, vision and values; and no sense of direction for the board itself, nor knowledge of your purpose, why the organization exists, and what sets you apart in your industry. Some organizations have a mission statement, yet still suffer from Foggy Focus because no one has looked at the mission for years! The mission should be revisited every few years to make sure it's still solid, and that everyone buys in. And it should be retooled, as necessary, to make sure that it is meaningful and compelling. There are good missions and bad missions, missions that serve and missions that don't.

A lot of organizations don't have a vision at all. They don't have a sense of what they want to become and how they want the organization to grow five-to-10 years into the future.

This is Foggy Focus. And most organizations I deal with don't have a set of guiding values or principles to keep the board (and subsequently the whole organization) on track. This is also Foggy Focus.

So, how do we create **clear** mission, vision and values? It begins at the broadest base. Just revisit what you have. Make sure these foundation pieces are clear and accurate, and include the words and concepts that will guide you.

When I work with boards to help them create or revitalize their mission, vision and values, I encourage them to begin at square one. Through a series of what I call "defining questions," you can look at the organization from a very rudimentary point of view. Once each question has been answered to the board's satisfaction, the mission, vision and values flow naturally out of those answers. And while the questions seem very simplistic, it is *amazing* how many differing opinions come to the surface during the process. Then, out of the clarification and melding of these diverse ideas, will come a powerful sense of the organization's uniqueness, personality and value to the world. The process also provides a strong basis for strategic planning, and for setting goals for developing and improving the organization. Another benefit I've discovered from the process is that it creates a new cohesiveness among board members, and re-energizes their dedication to the organization's success.

Here are the defining questions.
1. Who and what are we?
2. What do we believe?
3. What do we do?
4. Why do we do it?
5. Who benefits from what we do?
6. What makes us desirable?
7. How do we accomplish what we do?
8. How do we know when we are successful?
9. Where and what do we want to be in 10 years?

While these defining questions appear to be easy to answer, the key is to get to a place where the answer is exactly the same for each board member, so let's examine each of them a little closer.

1. First of all, who and what are we? This is a brief, but distinguishing statement that clearly defines the scope of your organization. What you determine for this will have an overriding impact on the answers to the next questions. For example, if you say, "We are Amalgamated Health Services (or whatever your name is), a long-term care facility servicing the northern suburbs of Atlanta," you create a boundary that limits your vision of the future. On the other hand, if you identify yourself as Amalgamated Health Services, an organization providing long-term care *and aging services* to Greater Atlanta, you've now expanded not only your scope, but also your potential for growth and development in the future. While it is possible to define yourself *too* broadly, most boards I've worked with err on the other, more self-limiting side.

2. What do we believe? "We believe that senior citizens who can no longer take care of themselves, need a safe and nurturing environment in which to live." What do we believe? "We believe that people with developmental disabilities need support in the community." Define what it is you believe. "We believe that employees need a supportive, respectful work environment in order to provide quality service." These are the beliefs about what the organization does. "We believe that we are called upon by our faith to help people in our community find affordable housing." This can be a long list of things you believe and value. Then, from that are extracted five-to-10 "core values" or beliefs that will guide operational decisions and give the CEO and management a foundation for day-to-day operations and decisions. These core values also instill a renewed sense of pride and allegiance in employees, and usually include statements about quality of service, standards of performance, business integrity, fiscal responsibility, community relations, employee relations, spiritual foundation, organizational climate and leadership

effectiveness. Other examples of beliefs from actual organizations can be found in Appendix A.

3. Then answer, what do we do? I can't tell you the number of board members who can't answer that question clearly. What *do* you do? It isn't as simple as "we help people with substance abuse issues." You have to be more clear about it and describe the services you provide for those people. Board members are usually lay people, so they don't need to know the organization's business down to the nitty gritty, but they need to know what the organization *really* does. "We provide an outlet for young, untrained artists to display their talents." It's incredible that there are board members who have NEVER walked through the organization they serve -- a place whose existence and future rests in their hands! Every board member should be able to accurately describe what the organization does.

4. Now answer the question, why do we do it? If we "provide clothing for people on low incomes" why do we do it? Do we do it because we get a lot of clothing and we can't keep it ourselves? Boards must have a deep grasp of **why** we're doing what we're doing. Is it a spiritual "calling?" That's fine. But whatever it is, it has to be a common belief. It could be as simple as, "We do this to meet a need in the community."

5. Who benefits from what we do? For whose benefit are we working? Low-income seniors? Homeless youth? I want you and all your fellow board members to know whom you're serving. Are they inner-city veterans? Are they recent immigrants from Africa, Russia or Laos? Do you know the face of the people you're serving. It's so important. It is difficult as a board member to make the right decisions if you don't have a clear sense of whom you are serving. It is also important to expand your thinking on this topic, and take into account the "other" beneficiaries and stakeholders beyond the people who actually *use* your services. Employees and their families, for example, benefit from the existence of the organization, as well as the family members of those you serve. Other agencies may be

benefiting, as well as the community itself. It is important for a board to define together the reach and impact the organization has.

6. What makes us desirable? This question is not only important in helping develop the mission, vision and values of the organization, but will also be critical in strategic planning. This question is designed to engage board members in a discussion about the strengths and competencies of the organization, and defining what sets you apart from others providing similar services. In this process, boards will uncover their weaknesses as well, which can lead them to improvements in the way the organization operates, developing and enhancing some services or choosing to eliminate what they discover the organization doesn't do best. Once again, this question should be looked at from a broad perspective, not only focused on the client, customer, patient or resident, but also on what makes the organization desirable to employees and to the community as well.

7. How do we accomplish what we do? Is it through treatment centers? Or, do you have a bus that goes out and delivers clothing or blankets to the homeless? Maybe your organization employs social workers who provide counseling services at three walk-in centers throughout the city. However it's done, you need to all have a clear vision of how the organization makes the services you provide happen. And once again, the board doesn't have to understand the *details*, but just generally how the services are provided to the people who need them.

This question is also important in setting the vision and establishing the strategic plan, because it gets the board thinking about whether the organization is taking advantage of all the best avenues open to providing the services you want to provide. It will also get the board to begin questioning if there are new technologies or opportunities that haven't been pursued yet, but could help improve the organization's service capability.

You'd be amazed at how many times I've heard a board member admit, "I didn't know we did that!" after learning the answers to some of these defining questions. Something's missing if every board member doesn't have this information. And it's probably not the board member's fault. Communicating this kind of knowledge about the organization is the responsibility of management and board leadership.

8. The next defining question to ask is, how do we know when we are successful? What are our gauges of success? It may be, "Well, we know we are successful because we reach 40% of the indigent people in the greater metro area." Or, "The crime rate has decreased by 50% in the neighborhoods around our HUD projects." Whatever your gauges for success, it is the role of the CEO and management to help define them, and provide the board with the information necessary to assess that success. This is also a principal element in enabling the board to evaluate the success of the CEO.

Questions one through eight will provide the information you need to create your mission and core values. But that's only the beginning. The answers to those questions will also get you well on your way to creating an effective and meaningful long-range plan. Another very *significant* benefit is the sense of joint purpose the board will now have about the organization. The feeling that everyone is "on the same page" will serve the board in countless ways as they govern the organization.

But there is one more defining question that needs to be answered before the "fog" clears and the focus becomes sharp.

9. Where and what do we want to be in 10 years? This is the "vision" question. For the sake of the mission, vision and values, this can be done in a broader sense initially and then further refined when the strategic planning process begins. This question looks at quality improvement concerns, changes in service and service delivery, revamping or adding to the organizational infrastructure -- in essence, it reflects the anticipated and fostered changes that the organization wants to make to become better, bigger, and more successful in the years ahead.

An example might be "We want to become the number one provider of home health services in Cooperman County" or "We want to become the employer of choice in the low-income housing services industry" or "We want to expand from a county-wide to a regional service organization." There are many, many options.

These Defining Questions, in and of themselves, make for a wonderful combined retreat for the board and senior staff. And the clarity and singular purpose that come out of an exercise like this, can also serve as a springboard to more natural, improved fundraising as well.

For ideas on how to create an outstanding mission statement, there are more than a million possible websites you can turn to! My biggest concern however, is that your mission be clear to everyone *within* your organization; and everyone *outside* the organization as well. It needs to tell people what you do, for whom you do it, the needs you are trying to meet, and how you're planning to meet them.

Your primary focus must be clear, along with the qualities that distinguish your organization. Your mission statement must reflect your core values. It must also be written in a way that will energize, motivate and stimulate the organization! And with all of this in mind, it needs to be concise enough for people to remember the main points and take them to heart.

But even with an incredible, clear and compelling mission, it is not enough to fully drive and guide today's complex organization. A close friend of mine who was the CEO for a very large public organization, once commented, "With the mission my board just created, I could invade Norway and get away with it!"

Missions are supposed to be broad concepts of who you are, what you do and why you do it. But an organization needs to create a set of guiding beliefs or values as well. Values-driven organizations are more successful and more resilient.

A set of values is inherently part of spiritually-based organizations. And while religious values may be a great start, they may be interpreted differently by different people, even within the same organization! So organizations need to make sure that the values they agree upon are then turned into relevant, simple statements that people can incorporate into their daily lives.

The board's responsibility, in conjunction with management, is to create those values. Then it's management's responsibility to make them "come alive" as they are demonstrated and *lived* every day within the organization. This is the "values-driven organization."

Now a lot of times these wonderful values are created, but then the board doesn't hold the leadership accountable for making them daily realities. It is NOT enough to create these values and guiding beliefs. You can't just say, "Okay, that's finished. Let's move on," and go back to business-as-usual. The board must further declare that the values agreed upon will not only be the foundation of this values-driven organization, but that these values will be **demonstrated** within the organization."

The bottom line for creating effective values or guiding beliefs is that they must honestly and actively guide the organization's decisions and actions. Once again, take a look at Appendix A for samples of Guiding Beliefs. In Appendix B, you will see examples of mission statements with accompanying guiding beliefs from actual organizations, which illustrate what I've been talking about.

Foggy Communication

Ineffective communication on the board is a huge cause of Foggy Focus -- guaranteed. Don't panic. You are not alone. Communication in boards from coast to coast is notoriously poor, not only between board members, but also between the organization and the board, and from the board back to the organization. Very often in these situations, poor communication is tied into technology, and the inability to communicate clearly and *consistently* with all board members, in the same way.

Not all board members have access to e-mail. Some who have access, may still not be comfortable with it or may not use it consistently. Not everyone can open attachments or unzip downloaded files. Organizations cannot make communication assumptions. They must weigh their options carefully before applying one communication method to all board members.

Another communication glitch that causes Foggy Focus comes when board materials are created and distributed from more than one source. Consistency, predictability, and continuity of messages will be lost unless **one** person is designated as the contact person for all board communications. The CEO's executive assistant is usually an excellent choice to fulfill this role because of the consistent, day-to-day connection with the executive.

And there's nothing foggier than a "dis-oriented" new board member, or someone who's been on the board for years, who has also never attended a **formal board orientation**. The orientation program is the most important informational tool to get every board member on the same "page." I've worked with many boards where an orientation program is available, but board members are not *expected* or *required* to attend it. There are also organizations where orientations are inconsistent and information varies from person to person, because orienting board members is not a *formalized* process. In either case, board members don't learn the same "basics" and the fog hangs over the board year after year.

Board orientation should be consistent for all board members, and **required,** Prior to agreeing to serve, prospective board members should be informed that they will be expected to complete the orientation within the first three months of serving, or they will not be able to continue on the board. This means the organizational leadership, in cooperation with the board chair, has to have a well-organized, formal orientation program that can be conducted often enough to accommodate the schedules of new board members.

A board manual is an essential part of a formalized board orientation process. Organizations must take the time to produce a clearly written, regularly updated board manual. Since most organizations now have access to computers and electronic publishing systems, this is no longer the arduous task it used to be. While any manual is helpful, a poorly-designed, slapped-together set of documents can cause more problems than it solves. Board manuals that fit neatly in a 3-ring-binder format can be easily updated for new board members and existing board members as well.

Organization of the manual itself is key because it's a human trait for people not to read manuals at all. Organizing it into quickly-identifiable sections will enable board members to find and read critical sections, and know where to go for information that is less critical. I have found that five major sections work best -- The Organization, The Board, Planning, Financial Information, and Meetings & Minutes.

The section on the **Organization** would include mission, vision and values, a brief history, and information about the organization's cultural assets and heritage. A brief description of the services and programs provided by the organization also goes into this section. If the organization is decentralized, information about the various service sites should also be briefly described. A broad org chart is important, along with brief biographies of the senior staff (including photo, title and responsibilities within the organization). This depends of course, on the size and complexity of the organization.

The section on the **Board** should be divided into three sub-sections -- Membership, Board Member Roles & Responsibilities, and Bylaws & Policies.

Membership would include a list of all the board members and officers, their contact information (phone and email), and the date they became a board member. Following that would be a list of standing committees and committee chairs.

The second sub-section, Board Member Roles & Responsibilities would include job descriptions, expectations and responsibilities for officers and individual board members, and a description of the responsibilities for each of the standing committees.

The subsection on Bylaws & Policies would include Articles of Incorporation and Bylaws, as well as policies that relate to board members. These policies would include board term limits, conflict of interest guidelines, board meeting attendance requirements, liability and insurance information, information that relates to legal requirements of the board, and policies that relate to board conduct.

The section of the Board Manual devoted to **Planning** would include the current Strategic Plan and progress updates, organizational goals for the upcoming year, and any other pertinent information related to planning.

Financial Information would include up-to-date financial statements, current budget information, description of current fundraising projects (including projections and goals), and a copy of the most recent Annual Report.

The last section of the board binder, **Meetings & Minutes** would include general meeting information, such as meeting schedules and locations, a sample agenda, and a brief description of how the agenda is created and how meetings are conducted. Minutes from the most recent meeting should also be included in this section. Board members often keep copies of the minutes from the last several meetings in their binders, for easy reference during board discussions.

In addition to receiving a board manual as part of a formal orientation, the CEO and current board chair should set up a meeting with new board members. This would serve as an official "welcome" by the CEO and chair, and an opportunity to go over any questions new board members have about the board or the materials they received. The official board manual, including all five sections, should be provided to new board members at least two weeks prior to this "welcome" meeting.

During the course of this meeting, new board members would each be assigned a board "mentor" -- a sitting board member they could turn to as a resource on any board-related issues. I'll discuss a few more of the details about the importance of these board mentors in the upcoming chapter on Altruistic Self-Interest, but the value of these contact people is immeasurable, and provides a more accessible resource to new board members, beyond the CEO or board chair.

A site visit to one of the organization's facilities is also an important part of your formal orientation process. It enables new board members an experience that more personally connects them with the services the organization provides. Whenever possible, it is also helpful and enriching for new board members to meet and interact with senior staff at the time of their site visit.

For organizations that provide services to people overseas, or those that interact with individuals on a one-on-one, or more personal, in-home basis, new board members can experience the organization's impact through a professional-looking video, DVD or computer presentation. While these presentations are often designed to promote organizational fundraising, they can also serve as an excellent orientation or recruiting tool for new board members.

But however you do it, a formal orientation program works wonders for clearing Foggy Focus in new board members.

Foggy Purpose

Foggy Focus can be created whenever a board project or action has an unclear **purpose**. Very often, I have seen board members assigned to vague, amorphous tasks. The board decides collectively what they want to achieve, it is assigned to a committee, or a committee is formed, but the committee isn't given a clear sense of purpose, of what they're expected to do.

Let me give you an example. Let's say the board wants to determine the feasibility of buying a new bus for the organization. The task is assigned to a committee, and they're expected to do everything. Instantly, the fog rolls in, and you have a mistake just waiting to happen.

To prevent Foggy Focus, the board should assign a **purpose** along with the task, a "mini-mission" if you will. The board should tell the committee what the purpose of the bus is, what service it will provide, for whom, what goals it should achieve, and any other specifics about what this bus needs to do for the organization. The board is responsible for coming up with the answers to "What?" and "Why?" before it's assigned to a committee. The committee should then be responsible for determining the "How?" of the assignment.

When there is a lack of commitment or clarity to the project's purpose, the committee will not have a full understanding, and it jeopardizes chances for anyone developing any real *passion* for the project. All too often, this Foggy Focus yields an incomplete, partially-developed, and generally mediocre result -- not to mention the fact that it can lead to a misuse of committee time, and ultimately a feeling on the part of committee members that their time has just been wasted.

The entire board must be committed to a project's purpose, whether it's looking at the feasibility of a new bus, or selecting a new CEO. Without a commitment and adherence to purpose, it can cost you dearly.

Before a project even begins, the board should all raise their hands and say, "Yes. We understand and **agree** to the purpose." They must agree on the "Why?" But instead, too often, someone just makes a statement like, "We need a bus." or "We need to build a new XYZ building." It's amazing, but it's human nature. There are dominant personalities on almost every board.

There are people who want to advance their own agendas, some who almost tick like a time bomb and put everyone around them in a state of "rush!" And there are those who are not committed to the purpose anyway.

It's often an "assumption" process. People assume they know what they're doing, or assume that the *other* person must know what they're talking about! It's also human nature to be taken in when someone speaks in a rather commanding, confident tone. Assumptions can lead you right back to that incomplete, partially developed, mediocre result. Let me give you another example.

A board member or a CEO says, "We need a new swimming pool." Okay. The assumption is that we all know what a swimming pool is, and we know how much budget we have (these are all facts). And so when we're done, we'll have a swimming pool, right? But what if we *really* defined what we were **doing**, instead of making assumptions? What if the board asked what the *purpose* was for this swimming pool? Is a swimming pool the only option? And if we go with a pool, what other purposes could it serve? Could it be a community resource as well? Could it serve the local rehabilitation services when our people are not using it? Could be connected to another organization? Is it possible to share the costs of creating and maintaining the pool with another organization or community of organizations?

All of those questions can be posed if you take time, at the start, to define the purpose and take the fog out of your focus. But we don't. We just assume a pool is for swimming. It's for our people. And if it fits within this budget, off we go, creating a swimming pool. Huge, expensive mistakes are made that way.

I once heard a story about a company that had to buy a new printing press. So they decided on the press they wanted, and made a decision to build a new building to house it. By the time the building was completed and the new press was purchased and delivered, they learned it would not fit into the building! To me, that's an extreme example, but it still represents the consequences of foggy thinking before a project begins. And that's why Foggy Focus is such a dysfunction.

But the biggest problem created by Foggy Focus is the time and money it wastes. Organizational resources are wasted every year on false starts or projects that don't work out. We have to back up and rethink. Projects, especially major projects that require major funding, must be clearly thought out in terms of their future impact, or we end up building something that doesn't serve the full purpose, and may require adjustments, additions or a rebuild sooner than would otherwise have been necessary.

Another problem with Foggy Focus is that it frustrates highly talented board members who feel no sense of success and gratification, when the overriding feeling is that their time is being wasted. And keep in mind, the number one reason people quit boards.

Foggy Focus demoralizes the board, wastes financial and human resources, and is actually a disservice to the organization. But it's typical for people *not* to want to spend the time on creating a clear focus. Everybody's concentrating on mission, vision and values right now, but improved clarity all around is critical -- like what's the purpose of your committees? I can't tell you the number of committees I see that don't have a clear purpose. And without a clear purpose, tasks get assigned to them that are not appropriate for their committee. But it's difficult to say, "Well, we're not supposed to be doing that," if there's no clear focus on what you *are* supposed to be doing.

The Legal Duties of a Board

Foggy Focus could also create an actual breach of law as it relates to your legal duties as a board member. Your three duties are: Duty of Care, Duty of Loyalty, and Duty of Obedience.

Duty of Care (also called Duty of Diligence) is simply to act as an ordinary, prudent person would. Duty of Care requires diligent, attentive and informed participation, and clear communication. You have to be interested in getting as much information as possible, so you can exercise the proper care over whatever you're doing.

Duty of Loyalty is to act in good faith and in the best interest of the organization. Duty of Loyalty also requires that you disclose any possible conflicts of interest, if ever and whenever they arise.

Duty of Obedience is your duty to act within the laws of the land, and in accordance with the organization's mission, bylaws, rules and regulations. This is another reason that it is essential to be clear in creating and communicating the mission, bylaws, rules and regulations. You need to know them. It is your legal duty.

Boards have been pretty safe over the years, able to hide behind all kinds of "hold harmless" legalities and "Directors and Officers" liability insurance, but the day is going to come when some attorney will successfully break through to hold a board or its members legally responsible for their actions. The consequences will be far greater, and the cost to the organization much higher than a board member or two simply "stepping down" in the face of a controversy. Boards today have to be more clear, more mindful and more diligent in order to overcome the dysfunction I call Foggy Focus.

7

Dollar $ign Delusion

Another symptom of dysfunctional boards that I've found extremely pervasive in my work over the years is something I call Dollar $ign Delusion. This is the belief that the main purpose of the board is to serve as a financial watchdog, overseeing management to be sure they don't spend too much, and making sure that every financial "i" is dotted and every "t" is crossed. For some boards, this becomes almost an obsession.

Dollar $ign Delusion is also a lack of understanding as to the full scope of what a board should be doing; the fact that (as I mentioned in the beginning of the book), the board is more than just a **Guardian**. Dollar $ign Delusion is a lack of real appreciation and understanding for the equally important roles a board member plays as a **Visionary**, and as a **Link** to the community. And it is also the mistaken belief that whatever the problem, the solution has a monetary focus -- usually that we need more money to solve the problem -- rather than looking at the possibility that we need more *creativity* to solve the problem.

Many non-profit boards across the country are under the misconception that their entire purpose is to give their own money, and find more money to bring into the organization. They believe that before any action is taken, the organization should wait until the money is there. Where money is concerned, there appears to be a real lack of creativity on the part of many boards. Boards need to explore ways to get things to happen *without* relying solely on a financial solution. How can they do that? Working cooperatively with other people or other organizations should be considered. Finding something that already exists and utilizing it to meet the needs of your organization should be examined. There are a lot of non-money options.

And if money *is* involved, boards need to look at creative ways to stretch those dollars, secure a grant, or somehow use that money in an efficient manner so the organization doesn't over-spend.

Dollar $ign Delusion reflects an old-school way of thinking that worked well years ago when life was simpler, communities were more close-knit, organizations didn't experience as many change issues as they do today, and when things didn't cost as much as they do now. A board could spend 90% of their time carefully guarding and guiding the funds.

About 15 to 20 years ago, when many organizations started doing strategic planning, most boards I dealt with were doing a rudimentary or poor job. Some weren't planning at all. Those boards that *did* plan, would often look back and see how little (if any) of their original five-year plan had been accomplished. Early strategic plans were nice pieces of paper with generally no commitment behind them. But to be honest, even with today's strategic plans, boards and organizations are lucky to accomplish half of what was originally planned.

Governance & Fundraising

So, what ARE boards supposed to be doing? Keep in mind the roles of Visionary, Guardian and Link, and they are applied in **two** major categories of board function: governance and fundraising. This is especially true for non-profit boards. Boards need to spend time on both, not singularly focused on bringing in (and worrying about) money. And while in my experience I know that an incredible amount of board time *is* spent worrying about money, my goal is to help boards realize the importance -- the critical importance -- of concerning themselves with setting the right **policies** and guiding the **future** of the organization. The board establishes the vision and values of the organization, while management handles the day-to-day operations -- structuring the organization to reflect the board's vision, and operating from the foundation of the values created by the board.

Governance - Defining, Deciding and Evaluating

The three functions of governance are defining, deciding and evaluating.

Defining

"Defining" at a board-appropriate level, means clearly outlining the purpose and business of the organization. It is defining how the organization is going to operate from a broad policy standpoint, as well as defining what the organization is NOT going to do and what it's NOT going to be involved in.

A very big issue for boards right now is determining where the organization really shines, what they do best and being equally honest about their areas of weakness. Sometimes it's a matter of learning how to stop trying to be everything to everyone. Charitable organizations, though well-intentioned, are known for trying to cover too many bases, and subsequently spreading themselves, and their funds, too thin.

One religiously affiliated social service agency I worked with did a brilliant job of reviewing their services in a very businesslike way. Their strategic plan delineated their weaknesses, and the board decided to eliminate those services in favor of promoting and supporting what they did best. Referrals were made to other agencies for services the board decided the organization would no longer provide. The board realized a very important principle -- that it is not detrimental to *refer* people to an organization that can more capably provide the service they need, and in fact fosters the notion of giving people the BEST possible service. Through these referrals, people actually received higher quality service, the organization was no longer forced to struggle along, and it was actually a greater demonstration of their desire to help the people they served. They were able to make a successful and dramatic shift from trying to be everything people needed, to more efficiently and successfully offering their best. With this new definition of who they were, quality improved and their financial strength substantially increased.

Just because an organization provided a service in the past (maybe since its very beginning!) it is the board's job to examine and reexamine the viability of all the services the organization provides. What you do, must be defined clearly. You cannot possibly fund the "everything to everyone" entity you'd love to create. And it is an important responsibility of the board to be that *defining* body, rather than merely rubber-stamping or validating what management defines the organization to be.

I worked with another organization that had allowed itself to expand to several additional locations throughout the country. They saw a need and believed it was in their mission to meet that need. Problems naturally arose with each additional entity, issues specific to their location and population. The organization was now providing central office services, and trying to connect with and oversee divisions thousands of miles away! Problems (and travel expenses) kept mounting. In order to maintain their new national expansion, they were faced with major funding issues. Dollar $ign Delusion sent them into a reactionary spin, searching for ways to get more money! They ultimately found themselves unable to financially solve the problems, and were forced to divest themselves of some of these new holdings. It was a very expensive lesson. Defining an organization on the basis of its geographical scope, is a very important, and often complex process. Many organizations, not just non-profits, have perished through over-expanding.

Defining is essential. It also includes defining who the board is, how they will function, what committees are needed, and defining what *they* are going to do in relation to what they expect *management* to do.

Defining is ongoing, and should be reexamined periodically. Defining is a powerful and important role of governance that is all too often neglected.

Deciding:

Deciding is the next function of governance. One of the fundamental purposes of a board is to make decisions. They are responsible for making decisions that guide the organization. The board makes decisions that determine where money will go, and decisions about who's going to be in charge.

Because of the way boards operate, one of their biggest problems is making good decisions. It is such a major issue, that it falls into another whole category of dysfunction which I call "Decision Paralysis," and which I will deal with in an upcoming chapter.

Boards make decisions about planning, programs and services of the organization, budget and finance, human resources, community relations and how they, as a board, are going to operate. In the chapter on "Minutia Mania" I will discuss these in more detail.

Evaluating:

The third major function of governance is evaluating. This is determining how successful the organization is, how successful the CEO is, how successful the board is, and determining what the organization should be doing in the future to improve.

Effective evaluating is essential to continuous quality improvement, but most boards I deal with have a difficult time with *how* to evaluate. And because the right gauges for evaluating the organization are not set up, the board often resorts to micromanaging in an effort to stay informed and in control. This very often leads to over-evaluating or over-examining the organization, is highly time-consuming, and creates major headaches for management, staff and the CEO. It also often leads to very subjective and inaccurate methods of evaluation.

More detailed information on evaluating the organization and evaluating the CEO is also available in the upcoming chapter on "Minutia Mania."

Being good at governance is knowing how to spend your time. Boards should concentrate on defining, deciding and evaluating, rather than discussing platitudes and worrying about where you're going to get your next big donation.

If you don't define, decide and evaluate well, the money won't be used properly. It's not good stewardship if you don't take care of, the "governance" part of the equation. Non-profit board excellence requires a careful balance between governance and fundraising.

Fundraising:

Fundraising is selling. And the key to making fundraising easier and more successful is being able to **clearly** define who you are, demonstrate how successful the organization is, and how well every donation is used. To do that, you have to go back to effective governance. It is very difficult to reach high level fundraising goals without it. I have sat in on many meetings where board members spend most of their time browbeating each other for not bringing in enough money. And yet they don't have a clear vision of what they're raising funds for! Invest your time in the governance piece -- defining, deciding and evaluating -- and the fundraising will flow naturally and successfully from there. The two go hand-in-hand. Clarity and efficiency help organizations raise more money.

8

Bigger is Better Fixation

One of the biggest board myths is a dysfunction I call the "Bigger is Better Fixation." This is the idea that the more people you have on a board, the more bodies, the better. It's the theory that more people means more participation. It's the belief that if you can spread the responsibility for decision-making around lots of people, no one has to take on too much. You can ignore board meetings when you want to, because someone else is bound to show up. It's the belief that the more people you have, the more dollars you'll bring into the organization. It's the belief that even if someone dies (I'm not kidding), that their name should be left on the letterhead because name recognition leads to higher status, and helps in fundraising.

In truth, the Bigger is Better Fixation causes more trouble, wastes more time, is obsessive, illogical **and absolutely undermines success**.

The idea goes back to the days when citizens became board members out of the goodness of their hearts, and organizations didn't want to impose too much on them. The more people who agreed to be board members, the better the chances were that there would always be enough bodies to establish a quorum and get business done, AND everyone could be tapped for a little money so more funds could be raised. On the surface, this seems very logical. In reality, it just doesn't work the way you thought it would, and in today's organizational environment, it's a diabolically bad idea.

There is also a belief that anyone who wants to serve, should be encouraged and brought onto the board. It's a feeling that if you turn anyone away, you may lose good people. The minute someone shows interest, you scoop them up and recruit them to be a board member, promising it will be a wonderful way to be involved in the organization. In reality, the larger the group, the more diluted everyone's input and impact is. The resulting feeling is that people's time is being wasted instead of valued. Big boards are more cumbersome, substantially less productive and very quick to burn out well-intentioned and interested people.

If your organization has been working for decades with a very large board, this concept may really be foreign and even upsetting to you. But I urge you to read on, to see how you may be able to turn this irritation into a pearl.

At a workshop I conducted in Florida, one participant argued, "A big board is good, because not everybody shows up; and that still gives you a good chance at having enough for a quorum!" I then suggested, "Well, if everybody *did* show up, it would be chaos!" What he wasn't considering is who *did* show up? Was it the same group of people attending meeting after meeting? Why were they showing up and what were they getting accomplished?

Giant boards may have worked in the days when boards had less to do. But today, they are a critical and integral function of the organization, and the board of directors needs to be comprised of a relatively small, consistent, committed group of people who are dedicated to the efficient functioning and long-term success of the organization.

Offering someone a seat on the board has traditionally been a way to reward people for years of dedication or volunteering. It's an expression of thanks, and an extension of prestige as you put someone's name on the organization's letterhead. It's a way to help people feel important, and connect them socially with other "important people" where you can all say, "I'm on the board of ABC Charity." That is not the road to a high quality, highly-functioning, decision-making body.

Some boards are enormous in an effort to have representation from their important interest groups -- their men's and women's groups, an auxiliary, and major financial supporters. It's often a "reward" to be a board representative and have a "say" in the future of the organization. I've seen actual negotiations over board positions, where the men's club says, "We have x number of members, and donate over a million dollars a year, so we want three people on the board." They will actually argue that "If we're going to be properly represented, we need to have at least three board positions." Well, now you have three additional people on the board. And if you have four or five of these kinds of groups supporting your organization, before you know it, you have a big, inefficient, political board. A board whose purpose is still *supposed* to be defining, deciding and evaluating, but who choose instead to just act as dutiful representatives of their own sub-groups within the organization, rather than advocating for the entire organization. A board that's too big is ill-conceived in today's non-profit environment, unless you believe the purpose of having a board is to create a big pool of people you can tap for financial donations! Frankly, this is no longer a viable concept, and is in fact a detriment to the organization. We have to get people off this concept.

Some boards feel required to have representation from all the groups that originally came together to create the organization in the first place. Religious organizations, for example, may have originally pooled their resources to create a healthcare or human services entity. As many as 20-30 congregations may have been initially involved. They see the organization as their "baby" and everyone wants to have a stake in its success. If the organization chooses to express their appreciation by including one person from each of the founding congregations, you now have a 30-

member board right off the bat! That's the kind of traditional thinking that causes big boards.

The same sense of tradition and allegiance extends board membership to certain people or founding families. And while it's all well-meaning, it's bad practice in terms of the board's jobs to define, decide and evaluate.

I was conducting a retreat a few years ago for the board of a very large non-profit organization on the East Coast. They had an unusually large number of people on the board already, and continued to add more names. This is the organization that, as a matter of fact, maintained the names of their *deceased* board members on the roster! One of my strong recommendations to them was that they downsize the board considerably, and set up term limits. Tears began to well up in the eyes of a highly-respected, very involved, 20-year veteran of the board who lamented, "It sounds like the best solution is for people like me to resign from the board in order to make this possible."

I often get this kind of strong reaction from board members and chairs across the country, when I introduce the Bigger is Better dysfunction. Many have commented that they have been operating with a giant board for decades! And while they admit that it does cause problems, they don't know how to respectfully undo what many of them see as a tradition, without hurting feelings and alienating people who have been supporters of the organization for years! Here's where I become that grain of sand in the oyster again, when I say that if you want to be successful in the future, you have to decrease the size of your **decision-making** board. In a moment I will show you a way to keep the other dedicated people involved.

Let me give you another example. Another board I worked with also had a very high number of board members (close to 90). But after painful deliberations, and strong opposition, they made the decision to downsize. The biggest fear, in addition to discontinuing their established "tradition," was that fundraising would be severely hampered by having fewer board members, since they saw fundraising as one of their main roles. They finally decided, and over a two-year period, decreased their board to about 30. They are now raising **more** funds because they have not only improved their board's productivity, but they have redefined their mission and vision, and re-energized the fundraising process.

So what should organizations do with all those well-meaning board members who are no longer on the board? Here's an idea that works brilliantly. Remember, the only thing that needs to be downsized is the official, "decision-making body" of the organization. To keep the involvement of the dozens of other people who have served you well, and are dedicated to the organization; but avoid their having to be a part of the actual decision-making body, you create a Board of Advisors.

The board of **directors** is your decision-making body. But you can have an **advisory** board comprised of as many people as you can handle! I'll lay out the parameters of creating a board of advisors, but want to give you a bit more information about your important decision-making body first.

There are a couple important legal issues attached to the board - no matter what size it is. Remember: *every* board member is accountable for any decision made by the board. If you have 90 board members and only a small group of people show up to make decisions on behalf of the whole board, all 90 board members are still *accountable* for the decisions that were made. The board is a single, unified body. That's the part of having a large board that everybody seems to keep missing. Even if people don't show up, every board member is still responsible, and can be legally accountable for some major blunder of a decision that was made at a meeting they didn't even attend! This could be a frightening scenario for those suffering from the Bigger is Better Fixation.

When you have 90 people, and attendance for board members is not mandatory, you run into another legal problem, your responsibility to "duty of care." It's physically impossible to be diligent, attentive and informed if you don't show up to meetings! The board needs to be a reasonable size and people need to believe and know that their job is to be there. It is not enough to have your name included in the annual report, and merely add your personal prestige to the organization. You have legal duties as a board member.

So, if bigger is NOT better, you may be wondering what the optimal size of a board should be. I can tell you from all my years of research and practice, consulting throughout the U.S. and Canada, the optimum number of members on the decision-making board of directors, is from nine to 15. This idea is also corroborated by The National Association of Corporate Directors and a variety of other teambuilding and board development resources. And while a survey conducted by the National Center for Non-Profit Boards revealed that the average size of non-profit boards in America today is 19, it was not the recommended norm. From the standpoint of simple human dynamics, in the nine-to-15 optimum group size, there is also less social interaction that could interfere with efficient decision-making.

No matter how big the organization is, this is an ideal size for the decision-making board. This is key. It's a fearful reality for most organizations that have been previously fixated on having an enormous board. Can you have more than 15? Maybe. I don't recommend it, but it's possible. Keep the goal in mind. The board needs to be comprised of a relatively small, consistent and committed group of people who are dedicated to the efficient functioning and long-term success of the organization. They must effectively define, decide and evaluate -- together as one unified body.

One organization I know of has a 21-member board. They do fairly well, but not everyone shows up for every meeting, so they do have that problem. Any less than nine (if you get really excited about this and want to go even smaller) creates the potential for a small faction to run the organization. I do not recommend that. It sets up a situation where people can represent their own interests rather than doing what's best for the organization. You don't want less than nine. Fifteen is an optimum. I also strongly believe it should be an odd number, as it makes voting issues a little easier.

If it sounds like I am belaboring this point, I would just like to say, that out of **all** the suggestions I make to encourage boards to improve themselves, reducing board size is met with the MOST RESISTANCE. It can take *years* before a board decides in favor of downsizing. No one wants to give up power. And if you don't have term limits, it becomes even more problematic because you cannot even rely on attrition to create healthy turnover.

The following 12 points are designed to help convince the holdouts that the benefits of an optimum-sized board far outweigh any of the traditional viewpoints of "Bigger is Better."

1. Quicker and more lasting decisions

One of the biggest problems I run into (although it's such a common problem that people find it humorous every time I mention it in a workshop), is the 30-member board where 15 members show up. They make decisions, and then at the next meeting, a couple *different* members come in, want to rehash the decisions that were made at the previous meeting (the one they *didn't* attend), and suddenly feel the need to weigh in on an issue. And what happens, all too often, is that decisions get **un**done, or re-done! What makes it so funny is that 1) It's almost universally true, and 2) It's so obviously ludicrous! Time is wasted and progress is undermined. To avoid this, all members need to be there. Attendance must be mandatory! And if a board member must be unavoidably absent, they need to support any decisions that were made in their absence.

A board of nine-to-15 members will be more apt to come, take their jobs seriously, and make decisions that are well thought out and longer lasting.

2. Better mission focus

It is easier to get a group of 15 people to understand the organization's mission in a clear, collaborative way (and remember I said collaboration is a key to the future), than it is to try that with a group of 30 or 90! The larger the group, the more differing views of the mission you're going to have. And while everyone shouldn't agree on everything (it is healthy for a board to get *some* disagreement from time to time), it is essential that the mission be a common thought -- a common purpose.

3. Greater member involvement

An amazing psychological reality is that the smaller the group of people, the more dedication they each feel to being actively involved. With nine-to-15 people, there is a stronger sense of responsibility and feeling of "If I don't do this, who else will?" In a larger group, it's much easier to assume that someone else will step up to the plate, especially with 50 members on the board! The smaller the group, the more cohesive, dedicated and involved they will be.

4. Better informed body

This is probably one of the most important benefits of a smaller board. It is just much easier to get the same information to 15 people, than 30. It's just logistically and logically easier.

5. More uniform and consistent communication

If you have staff people working to communicate with the board, and board members need to call in for clarification, it is a lot less expensive, time consuming and cumbersome to deal with the needs of 15 people (or maybe just a few of them who have questions), than it would be to keep track of making sure 30 or more people all have the same, clear message. A smaller board is just better business. And board members are legally *obligated* to be informed (Duty of Care).

6. More rewarding and productive meetings

With over 25 years experience in meeting management, I can state unequivocally that meetings are more productive with smaller numbers of people. There are less people to be disruptive, (and even traditionally disruptive people behave better in a smaller group), a greater allegiance and understanding among people, and better overall team function. Teamwork is the key to productive meetings. So it's just logical that the smaller the group, the greater the potential for successful meetings.

7. Greater synergy and team spirit

It is very hard to create team spirit in a group of 50 people (unless you have cheerleaders on the sidelines). And when there's no continuity about who is going to show up for any given meeting, synergy is often lost. Smaller groups bond with each other and rise to the challenge of making the organization a greater place.

8. Greater inter-member accountability

The beauty of a small group is that they feel a greater sense of allegiance to each other, because they have the opportunity to know each other better. They see one another at every meeting, so the connection is stronger. They don't even have to *like* each other that much, but a sense of allegiance is *naturally* generated. And many times, what develops in these board members is something I call "interpersonal guilt." This is the feeling that "I better do a good job because these people are close to me and they're counting on me." In a 30- or 40-member board, it is much easier for people to remain anonymous. There is not the same sense of connection and responsibility to each other. This is an incredibly powerful tool for team decision-making. And a board should really be an example of group decision-making at its best.

9. Less micro-managing and meddling into operations

People who have a tendency to interfere with organizational operations are on better behavior when they feel they're being watched by someone who knows them. On a very large board, you might never know a board member is calling staff, showing up on the premises, or sticking their nose in all kinds of non-board-appropriate areas. There's no direct connection to the degree that there is with a smaller board. And with a smaller group, the expectations of what is and isn't appropriate board behavior, can be laid out more clearly, and maintained better by board leadership.

When there's a looseness or distance in their connections with each other, board members can misbehave and stay "under the radar." They are also not as concerned with what the other board members may think of their micro-managing. A smaller group is just generally a more well-behaved group of people.

10. Enhanced board image

As I mentioned earlier in the book, it is my belief that one-third of a board's job is to serve as a "link" to the community, and the larger the board, the less coordinated and consistent they are in this role. Larger boards are naturally a more divergent and splintered group, so the public does not always get an image of board members as a unified group, reflecting the best of the organization.

A smaller, coordinated team of people, who share the same organizational vision, will project a uniform sense of class and quality. When you meet those board members in the community, you will know the organization by the confidence and pride they project, and the organization's image will resonate and reflect well in the community.

If you are a multi-million dollar funding source and you meet a board member at a social event, your chances of donating to that organization are a whole lot greater if your impression is that the board member represents a clearly unified group of people -- a small, 15-member group that knows what they're doing in terms of governing this organization. A person who has been on the board for many years, in a more superficial, less-involved fashion, does not serve as a good link to the community, nor to large funding sources.

A small, tightly-knit group enhances the image of the organization. Board members who are involved will represent the organization more intelligently, and people will see and *feel* the quality on every level.

11. More attractive to community leaders

A common, but mistaken belief is that the larger the board, the greater your potential is for tapping the "movers and shakers" in your community. Actually, nothing could be further from the truth. Top leaders want to be on boards where their input *counts*, and where their work can directly affect the organization's success. The smaller the board, the more attractive it is to top leaders.

The number one reason people quit volunteering is because they feel their time is being wasted. So, if you want major corporate executives and well-connected people on your board, they won't stay involved if the board isn't functioning well. A smaller group is going to be far more attractive for the person who wants to have an active, positive and impressive impact on the organization and the community.

12. Highly improved board member satisfaction

Member satisfaction comes from people feeling their ideas and contributions are valuable, and their time is being well spent. Big boards waste time by their nature. Board members who are satisfied, stay.

Okay. So what do we do with all these wonderful and noble people who previously served on a big board? As I mentioned, a very valuable option is to create a Board of Advisors. This is a **non**-decision-making adjunct to the organization and can include all your past board members (whose terms are completed), valuable volunteers, civic leaders and donors who want to have more influence on how their donation is used. It can also include people you may be grooming to invite onto the board at some time in the future, or people who are "testing" their own desires to be helpful and involved. These are ideal people for a board of advisors.

How you create this board of advisors is not difficult.

Define Your Purpose:

There are a number of purposes this type of advisory group serves.

1. First of all, they provide an important link to the community and the people served by the organization, by providing input to the board of directors on the needs and reactions of the community and other stakeholders.

2. Creating this type of a group also maintains the commitment and involvement of past board members, and provides a well-informed volunteer base for committees and other special projects.

3. It also serves as a kind of training opportunity for people who would like to be board members in the future.

4. Creating a board of advisors also provides a fundraising resource.

5. It can also be an excellent communication tool for reaching the community through respected opinion leaders.

Membership:

As terms expire for sitting board directors, they earn automatic membership on the board of advisors if they wish to continue to serve the organization.

People wishing to serve on the board of advisors, who were NOT previously members of the board of directors, can be elected by a majority vote of the board of directors, when they hold their annual elections.

Each member of the board of advisors is then assigned to a member of the board of directors (with the exception of the board chair). Each director serves as an official "contact person" to provide an ongoing communication link between the two boards. So, if you have 98 people on your board of advisors, and 15 Members on the board of directors, each Director would be the contact person for seven (7) Advisors.

- Members of the board of advisors receive a quarterly newsletter (in executive summary format) to keep them informed and involved. It is essential that some form of formal communication, specifically designed for the board of advisors, go out periodically. If the board of directors does not keep the board of advisors informed regularly (quarterly is fine), many of the board of advisors will begin to perceive this as an artificial entity without real purpose. Not only will they lose interest, but these feelings will also have a negative effect on their image of the organization. The important point here is not to create a board of advisors if you don't plan to put time and a little money into keeping them involved and enthusiastic.

- They serve **3-year** terms, with a maximum of five (5) consecutive terms. And anyone completing the maximum membership of 15 years on the board of advisors automatically retires with "emeritus" status (or other honorary designation) for life.

- This board of advisors should be comprised of people who represent the demographics of the community served, and any potential expansion areas. Representatives of the people you serve, and their families should also be included on this board of advisors.

Membership Expectations:

- Only one (1) collective meeting per year needs to be held for the board of advisors. It should be held in conjunction with the annual board of directors meeting, so that the directors can attend the board of advisors meeting and validate this important group of organizational supporters.

- A formal orientation presentation about the organization should also be conducted for anyone serving on the board of advisors who has not previously served on the board of directors.

- Beyond their annual participation in the organization's fundraising activities, some organizations expect each member of their board of advisors to contribute a reasonable, pre-determined amount of money to the organization each year, although this is not mandatory.

So, once the board of advisors is created, AND you have the size of your board of directors down to a reasonable nine-to-15 members, there are a few other considerations for making your board more productive.

Limited Terms

I believe in the power of **limited terms**. No matter how dedicated a board member is, the only way to keep a constant influx of fresh new people and ideas coming into the board is by limiting the terms of board members. The effectiveness of the organization and the board rests in the blend between dedicated, knowledgeable, experienced board members, and excited, new, eager ones. New board members are very valuable assets to the organization; so are more experienced members. Striking this balance keeps the organization vital.

A limit of nine to 12 years is optimal. Three three-year terms is a minimum (if you can get people to stay). New board members don't usually reach their full potential until they've completed one full three-year term. It takes time to know the organization, understand where the board member fits in best, and hit their stride. Their best contributions are likely to be made in the second and third terms.

If you let people go beyond 12 years (four consecutive three-year terms), you will tend to run into problems. Not only does it limit the flow of new people coming in, but established board members often become *entrenched*, and less effective. Three or four consecutive terms of three years each, is optimal.

Compulsory Attendance

And (here I go again, speaking as that irritating grain of sand), I also believe that **compulsory attendance is essential**. The duty of care and the important decisions that boards have to make really requires that everyone attend **every** meeting. Board members of yesteryear could come in and check the budget once a year. Being a board member today is an ongoing involvement in the future and success of the organization. People need to be told, **before** they commit to being a member of the board of directors, that they are expected to attend x number of meetings per year. This should be written into the bylaws or a written board policy.

The consequence for not attending should be very clear. If someone cannot come to all of the scheduled board meetings, or chooses not to, they need to get off the board. They need to resign and allow someone else to come in who is willing to get involved and stay involved. If there is an emergency, a member is certainly allowed to miss a meeting, but someone needs to be informed of the situation *before* the meeting starts. One miss per year should be allowed, unless the board chair sees that there's something dire -- a death, family health issues, or other crisis that cannot be averted. And if you must miss a meeting, that board member still has the obligation to stay aware, informed and supportive of the decisions that were made. Even one board member, coming unprepared or "out of the loop" at the next board meeting, can compromise the progress and success of the entire board!

Frequency of Meetings

In terms of how many meetings people should be expected to attend, I believe the optimum is **seven meetings a year** -- one every two months, plus one annual meeting. This is not unreasonable for scheduling people, and most boards can get everything else done through committees that meet between times. The full board should only have to meet seven times a year, with an option to call a special meeting in case of emergency or some critical issue affecting the organization.

Meeting more often is fine, but may be increasingly difficult to coordinate with everyone's busy schedules. Meeting *less* often can be dangerous for a number of reasons. It makes it more difficult for the board to stay informed, and requires a greater amount of "catch up" each time a meeting does occur. This can undermine the efficiency of the board. With the complexity of today's organizations, there is just too much business to be done. If the board or committees don't have the opportunity to address these needs in a timely way, management will have to fill the void. More decision-making power in the hands of management may be inappropriate, and not in the best interest of the organization.

Formal Orientation

As I mentioned, within the first three months of anyone's membership on the board, and preferably *before* they are inducted officially, I think it should be mandatory that new board members attend **a formal orientation program**. It should be an absolute condition of board membership, not optional. Many organizations I know design wonderful orientation programs that board members just never quite have the time to attend. That is a huge mistake. Elements of a good orientation program are covered in detail in Chapter 6 on the dysfunction of Foggy Focus.

Annual Enrichment

Every year the board needs an opportunity to learn more about the organization and explore ways they can improve how they work together. This is all a part of an **annual enrichment program**. When boards work on improving themselves, they are able to more competently serve their organization. The board development function continually looks at ways to be the best possible board. Either through a separate committee or part of the Executive Committee's tasks, a pre-approved annual program is planned for improving board function. Investing in an educational and motivating board development retreat each year will reap more creative, successful and financial benefits to the organization. It is money well spent, and boards should not feel guilty investing in themselves, for the purpose of improving the organization's future.

Whether the board hires outside experts, chooses to tap existing management and staff, or calls upon the skills and wisdom of individual board members to help in improving the board, it is absolutely essential that boards take on the task of self-improvement.

Board Member Selection

And the last key to improving board productivity is creating an effective **process for board member selection**. Look for people with qualities that will benefit the board. Structure the board in terms of representation and respect to your constituencies. Remember the board's role as a "link." Consider the qualities and demographics that will link you to the geographic community where the organization is located, and the qualities that will link you to the community you serve. Both are essential to the board. In the next chapter we will take a more thorough look at board member selection.

9

Dysfunctional Diversity

And since we're on the topic of board member selection, the next symptom of dysfunctional boards I've discovered is what I call "Dysfunctional Diversity." This is a very common situation, where boards tend to be filled with a lot of the same kinds of people -- friends and family members of current board directors, and people generally from the same socio-economic level. The tendency to look for *new* board members from within your well-established peer group only becomes a problem when you consider that fully one third of the board's purpose is to make sure the organization is responsive to the community and the people it serves -- the "link" role introduced in Chapter 4. So, by looking for new board members among old friends or family members, what is created is a very homogeneous board. And while this system worked well for many, many years, it limits the scope of the board today and their ability to represent all of the constituencies of the organization.

With the growing diversity of people and cultures spreading across the U.S. and Canada, there is a very good chance that your community has grown and changed as well, and a high probability that the old-fashioned method for bringing in new board members will no longer represent that diversity. From a fundraising standpoint, if your board is populated with socioeconomically similar people who don't have a lot of connection to wealth, it becomes even more critical to stretch -- to go outside your circle of comfort -- to meet the goal of serving as the best possible "link" to the community. This gives the organization an even greater chance at success.

I knew of a 50-member board, all of whom were financially "comfortable" and moved in a relatively small social circle. When they decided they wanted to bring a wealthy person on the board, they had a problem. No one knew anyone outside their socio-economic circle!

To solve the problem of Dysfunctional Diversity, a plan must be created for identifying, finding and recruiting people who will have the greatest benefit to the board, based on their knowledge and capabilities, social connections, and/or the constituencies and stakeholders they represent.

Work - Wisdom - Wealth

There is a well-known idea that every board should have a balanced representation of work, wisdom and wealth -- those people who are willing to give a lot of their time, those who are willing to share their wisdom in various areas (legal, financial, public relations, architecture, general contracting, etc.), and people who are willing to give of their own wealth or who may have some influence within a group of very wealthy people. Those are the three major contributions to the board, and all three are necessary for a board to be successful and balanced.

Another type of board representation needed, is someone who serves as a representative of a major constituency. This often falls under the category of "wisdom," as they can offer the board a critical and necessary perspective, and insight into the potential reaction of the organization's constituency to any board-created policy and/or change within the organization. Naturally, they may also contribute in the areas of work or wealth.

I worked with one board a couple years ago that was all work. They were lovely, wonderful people, church buddies that bonded together to be on the board of this organization. They were willing to just work their tails off. But without that balance -- without the addition of the specific wisdom the board needed, and connection to some of the wealthier members of their community, they were not able to rise to the level of success they wanted for the organization.

That's not to say that there wasn't great wisdom among the existing board members, but not the specific *kind* of wisdom the organization needed. There wasn't a legal expert on the board, or someone who was financially knowledgeable. And both of those skills were badly needed in order for the organization to grow and develop.

Some board members are willing to serve on any committee you need. They have the time to do it, and they may have some wisdom as well, but to achieve the highest effectiveness of the board and the success of the organization, you have to seek out new board members, people who have expertise, *specialized* information or a *specialized* perspective.

The "wisdom" we're talking about here means any kind of valuable knowledge that the board needs on an ongoing basis, and doesn't have. All kinds of wisdom can be beneficial. In a nursing home, for example, the wisdom of a resident may be very valuable. But it's important for the board to 1) look at what is needed, 2) assess the wisdom already available within the organization, and 3) assess whether it is more feasible to use an outside, paid consultant for certain types of wisdom, rather than occupy a board position just for that purpose. Then, you can actively seek out people with the specific wisdom you need.

On one particular rural board, almost every board member was involved in the same business, running a farm. They all had basically the same wisdom to share. Then, whenever the organization needed other support -- legal, financial, or public relations -- funds had to be allocated to pay an outside expert to come in and advise them. The board itself did not contain the wider diversity of wisdom they needed. And when it came to wealth, once again, no one was connected or influential outside their immediate circle. The lack of *balance* in the areas of work, wisdom and wealth will undermine the success of any organization, no matter how good your intentions are.

Dysfunctional Diversity also happens when the board does not adequately represent the constituency and stakeholders who are vital to the organization and its future. A lot of boards are filled with great, very involved people, but when it really comes down to it, they don't *truly* understand what it's like to be the *recipient* of the services offered by the organization. They don't know what it's like to be the family member of someone receiving services. They don't know what it's like to be an employee. Boards need to address the kinds of diversity and influence that will make their boards successful.

Board Selection

Boards often also have problems in the area of "generational diversity." They complain that it's hard to attract young people. Boards are often comprised of older retirees, who have the time and desire to serve, but these people also come with a set of generational values, and look at issues from a totally different perspective than the young people they'd like to attract to the board.

As I mentioned earlier, the book "Generations at Work" addressed the values differences among four distinct generations. In my work with boards and board leaders across the country, this major generational rift is evident again and again. People from one generation tend to have a different set of values when it comes to dedication to the *time* involved in being a board member. Different generations have different views and display different values in terms of what they see as *important* to an organization. And if older, established board members don't make a concerted effort to encourage and embrace newer, younger board members, these young people won't stay. Many times in my experience, younger people have come onto a board. They are really what the board wants, but older members create an almost clique-like environment, shutting the younger board members out. And before you know it, the younger board members are gone. Why? Because they never felt welcomed or valued, and ultimately felt their time was being wasted.

The biggest cause of Dysfunctional Diversity on a board is the traditional belief that the best way to get new board members is simply to "ask people." There's a popular (and dysfunctional) notion that you should ask *anyone* who looks like they may be willing to be on the board! This is not a useful, purposeful, or proactive approach. Boards today must go beyond the concept of seeking out any "warm body" and proactively 1) set up **criteria** for what they're looking for -- experience, knowledge, skills, connection, 2) set up a **process** to find the people they want, and then (scary as it sounds) 3) **cultivate capable strangers**. Boards today must cultivate people whom they've heard (through reliable sources), will fit the demographics and characteristics they're looking for -- who fit the work, wisdom, or wealth and/or someone who represents an important constituency or stakeholder group. The organization will thank you for it.

It's time to **stop** the process of "Oh, I know someone in my congregation who could serve. This good friend of mine just loves to work and do fundraising!" (or whatever it might be) That would be great *if* your friend fits the board's pre-established criteria for what they need in new board members. But otherwise, forget it! Be brave, dig in, and keep looking. The "warm body" model just doesn't cut it anymore.

You may even have to do *research* to find some people. But before you begin, the most important thing is to take time as a board to clearly determine what you *need* and *want* on the board.

When board members meet people at the local men's club, or on a golf course, and begin looking at them as potential board members, you can end up with a board that's 99% men. The problem is the process. I know it's comfortable, believe me. But "comfort" will only serve you if the board's purpose is predominantly social. If the board's purpose is to get a job done, then your comfort will come from knowing that the board is well-structured, and led by a highly qualified leader. The leader is the key. And unlike the organization itself, which must very *carefully* monitor its hiring practices, the beauty of a board is that you can actively seek people of one gender, or in a specific age group, and it is not considered discriminatory or illegal. The board can actually stipulate, "We need more women on this board," and it's perfectly legal.

Another cause of Dysfunctional Diversity is the lack of an active, ongoing program to look for potential new board members. Current board members usually wait for that "uh-oh" moment when someone announces, "Three people are leaving the board in May, so we have three months to find replacements." And that's when people usually turn to the men's club or the golf course!

Setting Up Criteria

If you start from day one knowing that within a year, three people's terms on the board will be up, you can begin establishing criteria, looking for the exact people you need, and seeing who might be interested. You have time to get the word out through your various channels, and can ultimately do a better (and less stressed) search. People may even come forward because they heard you needed someone with their talents!

Some factors to consider when you set up criteria -- the key to creating the right kind of diversity on your board -- include age and gender. If you are an organization that serves people across all age groups, you need to have a wide age diversity on your board. And if you are an organization that primarily serves women, it is ludicrous to have a predominantly male board (although you'd be amazed at how that can happen!) Consider the gender diversity on your board. If it's off, review the way you select new board members and fix the problem. The intention is not to discriminate, but to consciously and thoughtfully choose board members outside the "buddy system," who can best represent the organization and foster its future success.

Now, for the sake of argument, regarding a board that's predominantly male, I must admit that I once came across a board that governed and guided a nursing home where all the residents were retired nuns. I was told point blank that not only was their board *comprised* of all women, but that it would *remain* all women. In fact, all the board members would specifically be nuns and retired nuns! The board had the right to make those choices, and they did. They knew whom they were serving, and defended their choice as a way to meet their "link" role.

And so you must continually ask, as board members come and go, does the diversity of your board help you fulfill your "link" role? And, just as importantly, do you also have the right people to fulfill the equally important roles as "visionaries" and "guardians" of the organization? The diversity of your board will also affect how the board collectively views the future, and the aspects of the organization and its history you will preserve and protect in your "guardian" role.

If you serve a major community that includes people at a wide variety of income levels, your board should reflect people from different income levels. It is yet another criteria by which you can recruit and select board members. A board that respects and reflects its constituencies includes representatives from major stakeholders, and support and interest groups. If you have a large building in a community of people who are concerned, confused or uncomfortable about what you do, you may want to include an influential community leader on your board. This strategy can serve to smooth ruffled feathers when the board needs to make politically unpopular decisions for the organization. This is especially true with organizations that have direct impact on the community as part of their mission, for example, urban redevelopment programs, or residential treatment centers.

You might want to cultivate people with certain kinds of experience. It might be a physician or an architect. A board today would be smart to recruit a general contractor to serve on the board, particularly if they are contemplating renovation or new construction. That kind of knowledge and experience can help the board maintain economy and efficiency on the project. Remember, you have only 15 total board members, so you have to be judicious in your diversity. Set priorities on what's important to the organization. If you can find one person who can fulfill several desirable diversities (like an elderly, female accountant), you have it made. You can also fulfill some of your stakeholder representation by inviting some people to serve on your Advisory Board, when there are no available positions on the board of directors. This is another excellent reason to create a board of advisors.

10

Turnstile Leadership

Affectionately known as "leadership roulette," Turnstile Leadership is the traditional dysfunction of letting everyone have "a turn" at being the leader. Once you've climbed the proverbial board "ladder," rung by rung, and invested a certain number of years of service, you get to be the leader.

In reality, leadership is the strongest and most important element in making a board effective, and ultimately, in making the organization successful. This is **not** about taking turns. That concept must stop! This is about **leadership** within the board itself, and the importance of how the board interacts with the leadership of the organization.

The old model started with an assumption that if you're on the board, you must *automatically* be a good leader, or you wouldn't be there, especially if you've served on several other boards! After all the years of talking to thousands of board members and leaders, it's amazing how many serve on several boards simply because someone heard they were on one board, and cajoled them into joining another! And it is true... you can become very good at being a board *member*, the more experience you have. But just because you're good at being *on* a board doesn't mean you'd be good at *leading* a board!

Turnstile Leadership is the philosophy that it will eventually be "your turn" to lead, either as a committee chair, one of the officers of the board, the chair of a special event or campaign, or (God forbid) all of the above. It does not speak to whether you're *capable* of it, have any *desire* to be a leader, or whether you'd be any good at it! There are well-intentioned people who have taken their turns as leaders and actually undermined the success of the board! Leadership is a serious consideration. Skilled leadership is critical! That doesn't mean you can't be a good board member. It doesn't mean you can't be a wonderful, active, wise participant. But we must become more realistic about what we want for the organization and how we want to achieve those goals.

All too often I have found that the weakest part of an otherwise competent board is a general lack of great, skilled leadership. Not everyone on the board has the potential for being a leader, nor even *wants* to be the leader. There's no shame in that. Face it. We have a lot greater need for large numbers of fantastic, skilled board **members**! Turnstile Leadership is dysfunctional and we have to get rid of the assumptions that surround this concept.

The dysfunction in Turnstile Leadership is also caused by a lack of a leadership development program. Boards need to understand that leadership is a *developed* skill. It is not an innate ability of people who serve on boards. Turnstile Leadership is also a problem with boards that do not have an active leadership *recruitment* process. Boards need to actively seek people with *demonstrated* leadership skills, who can be recruited as possible new board members, rather than relying on warm bodies or volunteers.

The keys to leadership on a board, and the essential qualities boards need to be looking for in a leader include:

1. Experience -- specifically leadership experience

Before you put someone in the role of board chair or even chairing a committee, be sure they have a résumé of demonstrated leadership experience. If they don't have leadership experience, but show leadership *potential*, give them an opportunity to develop their leadership skills by serving in a leadership role on a task force, special event or short-term board project.

2. An interest in the organization

A board leader should show a strong interest in the organization, beyond just wanting to be on the board. The best organizational leaders have a real and active connection with the organization and what it does.

3. Working knowledge of the organization

Leaders demonstrate a desire to learn more about the organization, and make an effort beyond attendance at board meetings. These are people who have perhaps volunteered in other areas, or who come to you because they've read about the organization (or the industry) and bring thoughtful ideas on improving your success. This is the person who continually shows a desire to go above and beyond.

4. An interest in, and knowledge of, your industry

I'm amazed at how many people work on boards, armed with a little bit of knowledge about the organization itself, but little or no background on the industry as a whole. I'm not saying that board leaders need to be as knowledgeable as staff, but the best leaders will have a broad working knowledge of the industry and how your organization stacks up within it. Some of these things can be developed in your potential leaders during their terms on the board.

5. Able to make effective decisions

While this is something that can be taught, the time required to help a person become proficient is a luxury the board can't afford. At the board level, this is a skill you already have, or you don't. And it's the kind of skill you'll be able to demonstrate. One of the great ways to determine this leadership asset is to give people committee decision-making responsibilities, involve them on a task force or give them responsibilities within a team. This is where you can observe their ability to make effective decisions. It's very important for those seeking a leadership position on the board, and is also a key method for developing leadership. Meeting management and priority-setting are two areas where decision-making is essential.

6. Financial savvy

Good board leaders need to have a real knowledge of the "big money" picture. They should be comfortable around financial reports, profit and loss statements, and have basic knowledge in the areas of investments and standard accounting practices. While board leaders don't need to be accountants, they must be financially savvy. And one way to learn this is to have a person serve on the organization's finance committee prior to their moving into a leadership role.

7. Team management experience and the ability to create cohesive groups of people

This is extremely important. Too many leaders and board chairs have a leadership style that unintentionally creates divisiveness. They don't encourage teamwork, and sometimes *create* antagonism between people! Some are bombastic -- it's just their style! Frankly, these kinds of people have no business being the chair. It is essential that leaders know how to "orchestrate" people. In the thousands of interviews I've done with board members throughout North America, a very common complaint is ineffective leadership that centers around the inability of the leader to help board members resolve conflicts and create a cooperative, team atmosphere.

In their book, "Primal Leadership: Realizing the Power of Emotional Intelligence" (Harvard Business School Publishing, ©2002), author Daniel Goleman and his colleagues describe the importance and significance of a leader's ability to create what they call "resonance." It is the ability to connect with people in such a way that they are eager to follow your lead and believe you worthy of your leadership role. "Resonant" board leaders bring out the best in other board members and inspire them to respect their differences and work toward common goals and vision.

8. Ability to communicate clearly, both verbally and in written form

Once again, this just has to be one of your potential board leader's existing skills, because it takes too much time to develop from scratch. Some board chairs I have seen through the years would have done far better to stay in their board *member* positions, due to poor communication skills. Some were very uncomfortable speaking in front of a group, while others never had a sense of when to stop talking! A good board leader is one who has mastered the art of clarity, brevity and energy in the way they communicate with others. A little charisma is a good thing.

9. Good human relations skills

Crusty or quirky board chairs are not charming and they're not amusing. They are also not effective! Unfortunately, there are still too many old-school board chairs who would prefer that all decisions be made by them and the executive committee. They intentionally alienate or intimidate people in an effort to make sure decisions end up in their hands. This is not leadership. Quality board leaders bring out the best in those around them, develop a collaborative environment, and cultivate leadership in others.

10. Respected in the community

Great board leaders are generally highly-respected people. The kind of high-integrity person who garners the respect of others is a primary quality to look for in someone you want as a board leader.

11. A sense of humor

As far as I'm concerned, if your board leaders don't have a sense of humor, it's going to be a long term. It is important that they be able to see humor and use it well. One board chair I worked with was a master. He had several trusty resources and was able to start every board meeting with a fresh, very appropriate (often industry-specific) joke or amusing story to share. A little bit of humor serves to lighten things up and gets people to realize that while what they are doing is important work, they should also enjoy the people and the process, and have a little fun! The best leaders never take themselves too seriously. They have a keen awareness of their limitations, as well as their strengths, and they project a humble, yet self-confident quality that engenders a feeling of trust in those around them.

There are exceptions to this... for those times when the organization is in the throes of making serious, major decisions, or when the board is dealing with negative issues, humor is not appropriate or desired.

Other than that, if you're going to *keep* your board members, then being a part of the group should be enjoyable and rewarding. Remember, we are not paying these people. They are volunteers of the highest order.

Another major issue that adds to the dysfunction of Turnstile Leadership is the pervasive nonexistence of any sort of job description for board officers, a lack of written performance standards and poor (or no) methods for evaluating board leaders. If people are not held accountable for how they lead, we will continue to have people take on the role, merely because they've put in their time and it's now their turn. Please don't misunderstand. These are usually very well-meaning people, but great leadership requires a specific set of skills, and without them, you can honestly do the organization more harm than good.

It is better to be a "follower" on the board -- a thoughtful, wise and devoted contributor -- and let the leaders be the leaders; rather than to *try* to be a leader because you were asked or because you were the next one in line.

Boards also need a mentoring program to help leaders and potential leaders get up to speed, and understand the needs of the board. This way, they are better prepared to take on the job when a new leader is required in any role. One board member I knew was just suddenly told, "We want you to be the chair of this committee." This was a person who had never been a chair, nor had ever had the chance to observe a chair and see what was required. Wanting to be as helpful as possible, this board member dutifully took on the task, and ended up doing a lot of faltering, wasting time and compromising the productivity of everyone on that committee. Not everyone *needs* to be a leader, and not everyone should be mentored into a leadership role.

And while there is still a pervasive notion out there that *anyone* can be a board or committee chair; and a widespread belief that everyone *should* get a chance to be in the leadership role; for organizations to be successful today, that role requires greater skill and savvy. Back in the days when the board chair was not much more than a presiding officer, there was no problem with different people "trying their hand" at the job. Today however, the most successful boards need a more formal process for cultivating and choosing the people who will be the best leaders. Emphasis must be placed on selecting people with solid leadership skills or clear leadership potential that can be tested at the committee level. Knowledge of the organization and/or years of experience is no longer enough.

There are a lot of large organizations, especially national associations, that take an approach I call "Consecutive Leadership." This is a process by which people move gradually into the leadership position -- secretary, treasurer, president-elect, president, past president and so on. While I think there is still a potential for that system to shift into Turnstile Leadership, I do believe that a lot of quality organizations use "Consecutive

Leadership" as a leadership development program. One national organization I've worked with for years holds a leadership conference twice a year. The purpose of the conference is to train their state and county leaders to advance successfully and skillfully into their next leadership role. There is tremendous continuity built into the process and the organization does a brilliant job of developing these leaders through the years. But part of it is the people who choose to come to that forum. These are people who have demonstrated an interest in taking on a greater leadership role, because they've moved into leadership within their local areas. If you don't have that kind of a development process, "Consecutive Leadership" just turns into another dysfunctional variation of Turnstile Leadership.

Another dysfunctional aspect of Turnstile Leadership is the fact that with this practice, you are sort of playing a game of leadership roulette. Through the years you are bound to get some leaders who are good (as good, dedicated people rise to the top), and others who are honestly not capable. The problem comes when that poor leadership sets the organization back, or causes good board members to quit because they don't feel well led.

Leadership is too often used as a reward for service. One person I worked with had been in an organization for years and took on the role of the chair like a mini-dictator, relishing the concept that, "Now finally, I get to be in charge!" The role of the board chair is a deep and powerful responsibility, not only to move the board forward, but to move the organization forward as well, and create the kind of environment where people want to be productive, and want to work together.

In Appendix C you will find examples of duties and responsibilities that can be used to create a job description for the Board Chair. I have also included similar examples to help you with the other board officers.

Term Limits for Officers

If you have a good chair, who is fully endorsed by the board, feel free to reelect that person. There has to be a limit though, to guarantee healthy leadership. In my experience, a good board chair, vice chair, secretary or treasurer can be reelected each year, for a total maximum term in office of three years in any given leadership position. Then, it's time for the current leader to step down or at least shift gears into a different position.

Some people really relish being a board officer, and if given the opportunity, would make a career out of it! They love to run things and are sometimes hard to depose. Meanwhile, other board members who might have considered seeking an officer position feel too intimidated by these powerful personalities, and don't even try. Unless there are established term limits, the organization cannot benefit from the fresh perspective that comes with a change in leadership.

From my own experience, after a total maximum term in office of three years, anyone in an officer position should be required to step down for a "sabbatical" of no less than one year before they can be reelected to the position they held prior to their sabbatical.

Yes. Good leaders are hard to find, and amazing things can happen with great leaders, chairs or board officers. But, if you create a system that allows even "good" leaders to stay too long, several things can happen. Long-term board leaders have a natural tendency to get a little too comfortable and close with the CEO and/or senior management. A healthy degree of professional distance is essential to staying focused on what's best for the organization. Long-term board leaders also unintentionally foster board member complacency, where board members no longer feel the need to develop or exercise their own leadership skills. And it can be dangerous for an organization if a bad leader gets in for the long haul -- either one who wants to essentially and inappropriately run the organization, or one who is a weaker leader and allows the CEO to have too much influence over the board. Term limits foster good governance all around. And truly gifted leaders are never too tied to the job not to allow someone else to try the reins for a while, knowing they have the option for reelection to board leadership after taking at least one year off.

11

Altruistic Self-Interest

Altruistic Self-Interest is another major dysfunction, very often caused by one person, or a small number of well-meaning people with the incredible ability to scuttle a board's effectiveness! Amazing as it may seem, it is all too common. The reason I call it Altruistic Self-Interest is that it is honestly done with the best intentions. It is done by people who mean well. But Altruistic Self-Interest is counterproductive and can have a tremendously negative impact on the success of a board. Let me give you a few examples of what I'm talking about.

The Benevolent Interloper

I have seen individual board members get inappropriately over-involved in organizational operations, to the point of micro-managing things that should be handled by staff. These are board members who actually go into the organization (feeling they have the right to, as a member of the board), and get involved in trying to improve the day-to-day function and operations. They truly believe in their heart of hearts, that they know a simpler, more cost-effective, or better way of doing things -- a creative idea, different method or new system that will **help** the organization. And trust me, the road to organizational hell is paved with the good intentions of board members like this!

For example, while attending a fundraising event for a charitable organization, a board member overheard two staff members grumbling about the number of overtime hours they were putting in during a capital campaign. In an effort to secretly *help* those staff members feel better about their jobs, the board member decided to talk with their department head the next day, independently "investigate" how things were going, and make a few "helpful" suggestions.

Altruistic Self-Interest should not be confused however, with board members who honestly serve as volunteers within the organization. That *can* work for everyone involved, providing the board member is willing to be *guided* by the staff member who is in charge. Board members who volunteer *take* directions. Those working from a framework of Altruistic Self-Interest have more of a tendency to *give* directions. It takes a very special person to be a board member AND work as a volunteer within the organization. The opportunity and temptation to share board information with staff during a casual conversation is heightened. Developing relationships with staff members is a natural spin-off from volunteering with them, but this kind of personal involvement with the staff can unduly influence board decisions that might affect those same people.

The Newscaster

Another common and serious flaw bred from Altruistic Self-Interest relates to board members who don't maintain confidentiality. They gain information from board meetings, memos or other confidential or privileged organizational communiqués and then try to utilize that information in a "helpful" way. In an effort to speed up the process, help things along or give someone a "heads up," a board member may speak off the record with family, friends in the community, or people they come in contact with inside the organization. The board may be considering changing the benefits package, adding a new service or discontinuing one that hasn't been so successful. All of these board considerations have an impact on people's lives, and "newscasters" often have a legitimate concern for the people who'll be affected. So, in an attempt to soften the impact that will be felt once information becomes public knowledge, they breach their responsibility to maintain board confidentiality and let information slip out.

Newscasters think they're being discrete. They may even tell YOU to keep it confidential. They may just *imply* that changes are afoot that they are not at liberty to disclose yet. And if they think their secret is safe with one carefully selected person, they are wrong. To quote Benjamin Franklin, "Two can keep a secret, if one of them is dead." So what so often happens, especially with bits and pieces of information, is that people put the pieces together in their own way, create a rumor that is often inaccurate, everything is blown out of proportion, and people are now affected by misinformation! This can have a powerfully negative effect on the organization and the people they serve. Board confidentiality is NOT an option.

The board is a unified body, and must speak as a unified body. Board confidentiality should be strictly adhered to until the board, as a whole, is ready to speak. Information doesn't leave the boardroom, period. This is powerful. You don't even tell your partner! In my years of working with organizations, I know that confidentiality is not a natural ability. It must be learned and practiced. Newscasters may even try to redefine confidentiality by suggesting that it's not a breach if you use info in a roundabout way, or only leak a little piece of it, just enough to help someone. But that's just not so. You are an individual and do not have the right to speak the business of the unified body. Board business is not your information to share. As a board member, you agree to be confidential. This is an important part of the job.

In some cases, board members deliberately use confidential information for personal gain, or to grant favors to friends or relatives. For example, if the board is considering a major building project and a friend or relative is a potential vendor for that project, a board member may give out advanced information so that person will have an advantage when the project actually becomes public knowledge and the bidding process begins. This is not only a breach of confidentiality, but could also border on conflict of interest. And in my experience, this type of newscasting is rampant and goes on more often than anyone realizes.

When good intentions go *beyond* what is professional, appropriate board behavior, you are deep in the dysfunction of Altruistic Self-Interest.

The Lobbyist

One board member of a senior housing organization had a dear friend who always thought it would be a wonderful idea to open up a hair salon right in one of the housing facilities. The board member agreed, and took it upon herself to ask the opinions of some of the people living in the building, and garner further support for the salon. Armed with the results of her personal interviews and the enthusiasm she had successfully built into the people who lived there, she went back to the next board meeting. At the point where the meeting was opened up to "new business," this board member began lobbying for her terrific, well-supported idea. An unexpectedly large amount of time was devoted to her lobbying effort and the board meeting was totally sidetracked.

While the idea of having a salon on site may have been very valid, through her precipitous actions, she set up inappropriate expectations for the people living in the building. This made it very difficult for the board to consider the project in a more formalized way, looking at the need for this kind of service and if it might be provided in a different or more effective way, or provided by a different vendor. If the initial idea had been presented to the board, prior to *any* conversations and implied commitments with her friend or any of the residents, this could have been the beginning of a very positive, productive, board-endorsed partnership between the organization and her friend.

Another situation involved a board member of a rehabilitation center. Years before, that same board member had a child who benefited from the services provided by the center, but saw that the equipment, while useful, was not state-of-the-art. Now, as a board member, he did independent research on the finest rehabilitation equipment available, spoke with the staff about it (since they were "old friends" from the years when his child was receiving treatment), and then went to the board with his brilliant ideas. He told them how to procure the equipment, and even how to do the fundraising to cover the costs! This is another example of a good idea, with great potential benefits for the organization, but handled through Altruistic Self-Interest, rather than through the proper board decision-making process.

Is it a good idea to make life more convenient for the people you serve and the people who work for your organization? YES! Unequivocally, yes. Those are wonderful, positive goals and the intentions *are* good. Altruistic Self-Interest rears its ugly, dysfunctional head, when you strike out alone, rather than trusting in the process of the board and considering the greater good of the organization as a whole entity.

Bright ideas, staffing issues and organizational improvements all have their appropriate places on the board agenda and in the organization's strategic plan. Board members should NEVER individually act in an official capacity in contacting staff, or represent the board to clients, families, outside vendors or agencies WITHOUT THE BOARD'S APPROVAL. Ideas for improving the organization -- whether they come from or through board members -- should be presented to the board, or to an authorized board committee, and approved by them, BEFORE promises are made or **any** individual board member takes any action.

Calamity Jane (or Calamity John)

There are also board members who become aware of a single negative incident within the organization and blow it way out of proportion. They make assumptions that an issue they recently heard about must be widespread and that nothing short of a full investigation should be conducted to deal with the problem.

A case in point happened in a nursing home, where an employee was belligerent to one of the residents. And while it was an isolated incident and management handled the situation appropriately, word leaked out about it to one of the board members. The way residents were spoken to, was something this board member held near and dear to his heart, so just *hearing* about the incident set him on a personal "quest." He began going into the organization and watching how staff members interacted with residents. It was unnerving for staff members who suddenly found themselves in an atmosphere where they felt mistrusted and spied on. And all it took to get this huge ball rolling was the action of one employee, on one day, who made one inappropriate comment, to one resident.

Now granted, there are important issues that need to be addressed within any organization, but you'll get a far more effective and permanent solution when they are handled through policy, and holding the right person accountable for solving the problem.

Board members may also hear rumors, or be privy to conversations, and if they believe everything they hear, it can trigger a dysfunctional reaction founded on Altruistic Self-Interest. Disgruntled employees may turn to a board member they know -- especially in small town environments where everyone in the organization, and all the board members, live in the same community. Instead of working through proper channels, investigating it through the CEO, the board member will start to do his or her own private investigation of the situation. This is just bad business. It gives illegitimate power to that employee, taints the reputation of the organization, undermines the bond of trust established between the CEO and the board, and ultimately damages the work of the board as a unified body.

It is not always easy for a board member to determine if a negative story or issue they've heard about is an isolated incident, or symptomatic of a real, pervasive, systemic problem. Boards must look to the quality of organizational leadership for the answers. If the board has a CEO they trust, and are confident in his or her ability to maintain a quality workplace, then any incident a board member hears about can be confidently, confidentially and successfully handled by presenting it to the board, and subsequently to the CEO. The CEO is then charged with investigating and should report back to the board. If the trust between the board and CEO is *not* there, the board has a right and the obligation to investigate any issue they feel could threaten the organization's welfare. These kinds of investigations however should always be done by the board as a whole, or by a board-appointed committee.

The Fanatic

And then there are board members focused solely on one issue -- people who align themselves with individual rights, diversity, fundraising or preventing wasteful spending. And while these are all noble, legitimate issues, the board's focus is supposed to be the big picture, not single issues. Should board members let their causes be known? Absolutely. Should they try to get the board to consider these issues? Certainly. But to continually bring the board's focus back to one board member's compelling issue, and gauge everything through that single filter, is not responsible governance.

Some of these people are crusaders. They have a pet project and have to push it on a regular basis. For some, the whole purpose of joining the board might be for a pet project. This again, is Altruistic Self-Interest. One gentleman on a board I worked with, joined the board purely because he felt the chapel in the nursing home should be rebuilt. His whole purpose was to get that chapel rebuilt and it was absolutely a one-issue deal. Feeling that the existing chapel didn't answer the spiritual needs of the residents, everything was centered around that whole idea. And while that may have been true, it was unfortunately the *only* thing he discussed, and it severely sidetracked the board and severely interfered with their progress.

Baggage Carriers

These are board members who have had a bad experience or know of one, and whose sole purpose for being on the board is to assure that nothing like that ever happens again. It could be that a relative died in a hospital operating room, and they bring that story (and negative experience) into all their board decisions. Some people may even carry baggage in relation to other board members -- people involved in long-standing disagreements, arguments, or still upset by deciding votes that may have been cast *years* ago. This kind of baggage then continues to undermine the abilities of people to work together in *current* board-related activities. It's sad. I have even seen personal baggage handed down from one generation to the next, where a son or daughter is expected to continue a long-standing feud! These are very personal, and major issues to those involved, but this kind of baggage is honestly petty and it is dysfunctional in terms of the board. When we look at the purpose and *business* of being on a board, we realize it's a bigger task and the good of the organization must override individual needs and differences.

Board members who carry historical baggage can have a significant negative impact on board success. One example I've seen on many occasions happens when a new CEO is hired. Board members who have had a long-term relationship with the previous CEO sometimes have major trouble adjusting to the style of the new organizational leader. This can often cloud their judgment and make them resistant to needed change. And while the guardian role of a board is very important, it should not block legitimate progress.

The Time Tapper

One of the most seemingly harmless, but truly counterproductive examples of Altruistic Self-Interest relates to board members who inappropriately drain staff time. While it is an expectation of every board member to be informed, that information should be obtained through proper board-sanctioned channels. Some board members though, take it upon themselves to request information or materials *directly* from staff, without board approval. They may contact staff members, requesting information about a particular organizational process or procedure; or to request another copy of a report they misplaced. Some call department heads just to talk about an issue or project they'd like to be more knowledgeable about before an upcoming board meeting. Some staff members have even been asked to produce individual reports for the benefit of a single board member.

What board members don't understand, is that when they make these requests, staff members feel *obligated* to comply. The CEO may not always be available for the staff member to ask if the request is *appropriate*, so staff time (and money) is suddenly shifted to answer the needs of an individual board member. It can also put the employee in a very difficult position if an important departmental project is delayed for the sake of fulfilling some request made by a board member.

If this practice is allowed to continue, it can be a major drain on staff time. That ultimately affects the organization's bottom line, and can interfere with the overall quality of service you provide. It should be made clear to all board members that any requests for information need to be channeled through the board itself, an appropriate committee, or through the CEO. Some larger organizations have specific staff members designated as the information liaison for the board. Committee chairs often have a pre-approved relationship with specific staff members they can contact to procure information for the committee. For example, it is not uncommon for the chair of the Finance Committee to have a close relationship with the CFO. But this is an acceptable, endorsed relationship. Anything outside those established, sanctioned bounds constitutes time tapping and is a very common, but highly counterproductive practice.

The Good Friend

Staff friendships are another big issue that can fall into the dysfunction of Altruistic Self-Interest. This is where a board member, through their affiliation with a local club or congregation, school, sports, family or any other affiliation, establishes a close friendship with someone who happens to be on the staff of the organization. This kind of personal relationship can totally cloud a board member's ability to make any judgments that might directly affect their staff member/friend -- salary issues, benefits, etc. -- all the things that boards have to consider. It can also be a potential breach of confidentiality. This is a big issue in small towns, where board members can't help knowing people on the staff. They may be the biggest organization, or the only one of its kind in town! Most of the people know everybody. But it is critical for board members to maintain confidentiality and remember that their job is for the good of the *entire* organization. They have a *legal* obligation to uphold the mission, rather than worrying about how a decision may affect their friend or cousin in the payroll department. Before anyone considers being on a board, they need to consider this, and be ready to make tough decisions that will affect all employees, for the good of the organization they serve, or they must be ready to declare a conflict of interest. One of the most power examples of this is when an organization must lay people off. This is an unfortunate, but sometimes necessary type of decision, and personal concerns should not get in the way.

The VIP

There are also people who join boards for their own personal gain. At first blush, they may look altruistic, but the degree of personal benefit they desire, tends to diminish the "altruistic" aspect of this type of person. These are board members who are looking for prestige, a way to make important business contacts, and a way to improve their own status in the community. These board members are *dangerously* dysfunctional to the board and often sit right on the edge of a serious conflict of interest. While they may not be directly selling to the organization, or directly profiting from board decisions, they are still there for the wrong reason. I have seen a lot of sophisticated examples of this throughout the country. Board members need to be there for the greater good of the organization -- for true group values, not for personal gain.

As I've described these different types of well-intentioned but dysfunctional behaviors, you can see that Altruistic Self-Interest comes in a variety of individual styles. But remember: as a member of a board, you are a member of a unified body. Any action you take *individually*, under the auspices of being a board member, NO MATTER HOW WELL-INTENTIONED, falls under the dysfunction of Altruistic Self-Interest.

Reasons & Remedies for Altruistic Self-Interest

The main cause of Altruistic Self-Interest is the lack of a formal board membership recruitment program, or a recruitment program that doesn't clearly explain to prospective board members exactly what is expected of them *before* they are asked to join the board. Letting people know what their role will be, using a formal job description, and giving people an honest sense of the overall gravity of their role, must be done to avoid Altruistic Self-Interest. Board members need to know that they will be learning some things that are different from what they're used to, and that there's a lot more to the job than sharing a cup of coffee every couple of months, while you look over the budget.

An ongoing board development program also keeps board members focused and on track with their proper roles and obligations. And a mentoring process designed to help new board members learn the finer points of their job is also a very important deterrent to Altruistic Self-Interest.

Ineffective leaders often allow people to go beyond their jurisdiction and meddle in organizational affairs. This also feeds into the dysfunction as individuals are allowed to stray into areas that are not board sanctioned, and monopolize meetings and agendas. Ineffective leaders do not hold board members accountable.

Advocacy & Accord - A Delicate Balance

As you look at ways to deal with Altruistic Self-Interest, it is important to recognize that you're not trying to create a board of people who agree on everything. That's not good governance either. A board's success is dependent on a balance between advocacy and accord.

You don't want to create so many systems, sanctions and accountabilities that you squelch all disagreement. Respectful disagreement is necessary. That's why you create a functionally diverse board. Advocating for one position or another on any given issue, and staying open and focused on doing what's best for the organization is the bottom line. You also want a board that can come together to achieve consensus on a critical decision. So there's a real balance needed and that's why you have to be careful. What I find very often is that the needed balance is *not* there. Maintaining that balance is the responsibility of the board leadership.

When there is too much **accord** among board members, you can end up with a "rubber stamp" situation, where nothing is questioned and future implications of a decision go unexamined. Even people who disagree, may tend to remain silent. This can have disastrous results. When there is too much **advocacy**, issues may be overanalyzed, people can end up "choosing sides" in an atmosphere that turns divisive, and important decisions can be dangerously stalled. When you are making values-based decisions that have significant impact on the organization, the need for total board buy-in and commitment to the decision, is essential. Therefore, the balance between advocacy and accord must weigh on the side of accord. This is a significant responsibility of board leadership, and is examined in greater detail in the upcoming chapter on Misguided Meetings.

With public boards / elected boards, this is even a bigger issue. To achieve the perfect balance between advocacy and accord, board leadership must have a sense of when the greater cause needs to take over -- when the focus must go back to the mission and values of the organization -- and the focus, once again, must be on accord.

I have seen this in many cases in my work with public boards -- city councils, park boards, charter schools, townhouse or homeowner association boards and other such organizations that are comprised of people who are elected to a governing body. Often, these people are elected because of their stance on a single burning issue such as zoning or redevelopment. Some are elected because of personal promises they have made to their constituencies, and these commitments and personal agendas cloud their ability to see the greater goals of the organization itself. Often, on larger boards, there is a tremendous disparity of values among the board members, creating a major imbalance between advocacy and accord.

I have seen this situation lead to rancor between board members, and a total inability to create joint focus for decisions that will benefit the greater group this board represents. While it is natural for public boards to weigh more heavily on the advocacy side, I have seen several create missions and values that have literally *increased* the desirable level of accord, and improved the quality of the decisions made.

To help board leadership in maintaining this balance, board members must be taught to act more as a team. They must have the ability to understand and gracefully accept disagreement, and the openness and respect to listen to the opinions of others before making a decision. Altruistic Self-Interest can lead to too much advocacy and undermines the potential for accord.

Board Member Rights & Responsibilities

In Appendix D, I have included an example of a document I created many years ago to help boards deal with several issues related to what might be considered a Code of Conduct. These Board Member Rights & Responsibilities are designed to outline the basic expectations each board member should have for the board itself -- what I call board member "rights" -- and the expectations the board should have of each board member -- board member "responsibilities." Within this document on the "rights" side, are the right to your own views and opinions, the right to be listened to when it is your turn, and the right to disagree. These are **advocacy** rights. On the "responsibility" side, are the expectations that board members will be open to other viewpoints and opinions, will carefully listen to all sides of an issue, and will work for mutual agreement. These are the **accord** expectations.

This tool has been very well received throughout the years by boards across the country and is designed to be agreed-to and adhered-to by all board members. It is also a tool for board leaders to use in keeping board members and the board as a whole reminded of and committed to these principles. This Code of Conduct is examined further in the next chapter.

Mentor / Protégé Program

One of the ways to insure that people understand the significance of their role as a board person and don't diminish or undermine it with personal issues, is through a mentor/protégé program. This is a program where every established board member is expected to serve as a mentor and take at least one *new* board member under their wing, at least every year or two. The mentor agrees to be available to that new person, and go out of their way to bring them into the fold so that every new board member is up to speed more quickly, and understands what they need to know to be successful. This must be done in a helpful, respectful, non-threatening and open way, so that your new board members are willing to ask questions. I've talked to many new board members who felt sheepish about asking questions because they assumed they needed to know everything the minute they came on the board.

A mentor/protégé program is a clear, open statement that new board members are **not** expected to know everything, and that questions are encouraged. Remember, one of the three legal expectations of a board, is that they be informed. It is their job as a board member, and the only way you can get informed is by creating a system that is open to people who have questions.

Mentors serve as advisors, role models and peers with successful experience on the board. It is their job to set an example, share ideas, and offer support and encouragement while orienting the new board member to the culture, employees, volunteers and strategies of the organization. With this kind of support, new board members have a chance to learn, develop their own leadership skills and involvement, and naturally become more tuned and committed to the organization.

12

Jurisdictional Jungle

If you could only solve one problem with your board, solving this dysfunction alone would make a significant difference in your success. This is certainly a pervasive problem, and I have yet to find a board that doesn't suffer in one way or another trying to hack their way through the Jurisdictional Jungle.

Simply put, a Jurisdictional Jungle is created when the powers and authority of the board, board officers, committees, the CEO and the organization's senior executives are not clearly defined. Organizations that suffer in a Jurisdictional Jungle have very loosely defined or undefined reporting relationships, authority, jurisdiction, accountabilities and so on. Traditionally, organizations have evolved by accident, rather than by plan; which is the perfect path right into a Jurisdictional Jungle.

First and foremost, the board has to look at their proper role and the appropriate relationship they need to have with the CEO. This is where most jurisdictional issues start. If the CEO reports solely to the board's executive committee, or to the board chair, this is not only ineffective, it can create major issues. The CEO of a non-profit organization must report to the board **as a whole** -- always. The CEO answers to the board. They are the body responsible for hiring and firing the CEO, and no relationship should ever imply that the CEO is accountable to any *one* board member or individual committee.

What is interesting about larger boards, is that in most (if not all) cases, they eventually defer decisions to a smaller body -- usually to the Executive Committee. So, in essence, the Executive Committee becomes a "mini-board" and exercises their authority over the CEO. And while this is certainly a way to be more efficient when you have a big, cumbersome board, the legality of it is questionable! Remember, the entire board is responsible for the decisions made by that Executive Committee. We must return to the concept of a nine-to-15-member board of directors with all the decision-making power, and remember that your "board of advisors" (which we discussed in Chapter 8) can include the larger group. This is the only way to cover all the legal, logistical and efficiency issues.

The jurisdiction of the Executive Committee, includes taking on the role of writing up the annual evaluation for the CEO, and dealing with direct issues such as salary negotiations, or some of the hiring procedures. But the entire nine-to-15-member board of directors, as a whole, serves as the ultimate boss of the CEO. The CEO can be *on* the Executive Committee (which is a good practice), but just can't participate when they're discussing the performance appraisal *of* the CEO, salary issues of the CEO, or any other voting that directly affects the CEO. But to allow any single person (like the board chair), or any small group (like the Executive Committee), to act as the ex-officio boss of the CEO is DANGEROUS.

I would also like to warn organizations away from using the term "President" for the person who chairs the board. It may feel like just a semantic issue, but the term "president" implies the real leader of the organization, like the President of the United States. Even Webster defines president as "the highest officer of a company." People feel a "president" has the last word, so to use that term for anyone on a board, is misleading. I strongly recommend the terms Chair and Vice Chair. In a non-profit organization, the "Chair" is the leader of the **board**, *not* the leader of the organization.

I was working a few years ago with the CEO of a very large senior services organization. The CEO admitted a bit hesitantly that at one point, the "president" of the board had chided, "Don't ever forget the fact that I run this organization." I just turned to the CEO and joked, "...with an attitude like that, I certainly hope your résumé is up to date!"

The CEO is hired to run the organization. The chair is elected to lead the board. The board is the ultimate governance authority over what happens to the organization, and it's very hard for a CEO to function if they have too many bosses. That's true for anyone. Without a clear reporting process, you end up in a Jurisdictional Jungle with splintered performance expectations for the CEO. And when you consider what the average CEO is paid these days, being trapped in a Jurisdictional Jungle is a major waste of money, as well as time.

You know you're in a Jurisdictional Jungle when boards permit individual members to exercise authority over the organization and/or employees, without board sanction and pre-approval. This can be extremely problematic. When individual board members call staff and executives directly, and give them jobs to do, you will find yourself in a Jurisdictional Jungle, overrun with Altruistic Self-Interested people! Getting out of the jungle requires that tasks or requests from board members, that require staff time, should be handled by the full board, through the CEO or an authorized committee that has an approved relationship with a specific staff person. The chair can be the day-to-day operating liaison with the CEO, but the bottom line is the CEO reports to the board as a full body. It is the **most important jurisdictional issue.**

Another common jurisdictional issue arises when committees are given assignments without knowledge of their authority and without clear goals. There's almost nothing more destructive than a committee run amok! Without jurisdictional clarity, they take their task, define it themselves and start to meddle in the organization, based on their *perception* of their authority and responsibility.

Maybe it's a task on determining the feasibility of a new building project. If their authority isn't defined **clearly**, they may run off and start looking at buildings, dealing with various people on the staff, and calling in contractors for bids. Not only does it take up time, but there may be implied commitments being made on behalf of the organization, by people who have no authority to make them! So it is very important that the board be clear about the expectations they have of every committee project, especially short-term projects, and the limits of authority.

Governance Power Models

In my experience working with boards entangled in Jurisdiction Jungle issues, I've discovered four (4) basic governance power models that tend to emerge. And they are, in this order:

Chair-centered: This is where the chair believes he or she runs the organization, is all powerful, and is prepared to exercise any and all power that the board relinquishes. The board may not realize they're shifting power to the chair, but they do; and the chair may be delighted to literally run the organization. If your chair is knowledgeable enough to understand the industry that the organization is in, they do less damage. But the potential for damage is the **greatest** in a chair-centered power structure. The CEO is more easily intimidated, and can actually be driven out. If you have an excellent CEO, this can be a very costly problem.

I have seen countless examples of this, and the main reasons it happens are that you have a person who needs the power (an Altruistic Self-Interested chair), and a board that is weak -- a board that doesn't understand their power and their legal obligations. So the chair takes over in the vacuum. This is the most undermining structure.

Board-centered: This second basic governance power model is where the board takes on all the authority, announcing to the CEO, "Everything has to be approved by us. You can't move without our say-so." This again can be a very destructive model, especially because it can hamper the authority of the CEO and create an incredible time roadblock as the CEO must wait for the board to get together in order to get anything approved and done! It is also incredibly time intensive for the CEO who has to continually make a case for everything that has to be approved.

CEO-centered: Here's where the chair and the board are basically controlled by the CEO, and the CEO generally views the board (and uses them) as a "rubber stamp." I've seen several cases of this kind of power, some in fact, where the CEO even selected the board chair! In this power model, the CEO calls the shots, and the board nods agreement.

In the olden days, this model worked fine, because organizations were not very complex. Survival wasn't as much of an issue as it is today and strategic planning wasn't nearly as significant. Organizations functioned the same basic way, year after year, so boards didn't need to be as involved overseeing the organization. A good CEO could handle things very effectively.

But that strategy doesn't work anymore. It is a mistake -- absolutely -- to let the CEO totally run an organization, with very little board involvement. And there is a *legal* implication for non-profits. There is less risk if the board is guiding the organizational decisions -- through Mission, Vision, Values and policies -- and it is just good governance. And governance is the **key** to honestly, efficiently and respectfully utilizing someone else's money, which is really what you're doing.

There are a few common ways this develops. One is through a process where a board that doesn't fully understand the amount of authority and decision-making power they should have, gives up that power to a strong CEO, and the CEO maintains this imbalance. This generally happens when a CEO keeps the board in the dark, carefully selecting what information is released to board members. These are often also boards with very little turnover. People are reelected due to careful management by the CEO. I worked with a group of top leaders at a national conference and one CEO was very clear about it. "This is my board," said the CEO. "I run the organization." Essentially, he just wanted the board to provide support for his leadership, and not interfere.

The second way this power model can develop is through a strong entrepreneur. There are visionaries throughout the country who have developed their own wonderful ideas, and created small non-profit organizations designed to advance our society or fulfill a spiritual mission, in an effort to enrich the lives of others. As the organization is formed, the entrepreneur usually selects a board of people they know. These are often people who support them fully, and who are honored to be part of a great vision. These start-up boards are often informal, legal documentation is minimal, and the mission, vision and values are sketchy, often existing solely in the mind of the visionary. These board members see themselves as a necessary support function to the founder, helping him or her realize a dream. These boards can be dangerously small in number, which adds to the allegiance they feel to the organization's founder. At this stage, a highly motivated entrepreneur is the driving force, the CEO and in some cases the *only* staff person. For all intents and purposes, the entrepreneur *is* the organization, so the board questions little if any of his or her decisions. As the organization grows, however, and is more financially dependent on donations from a greater number of stakeholders, the need for staff and other infrastructure grows along with it and the board's involvement becomes more important. And as the organization truly develops, the mystique and almost-absolute authority the founder has enjoyed during the initial phase fades.

As with any growing entity, the entrepreneurial organization eventually outgrows its creator and must develop an identity and a vision beyond the individual who started everything. This can be a painful and difficult process when the original vision grows beyond the visionary, the first executive director needs to be hired, and battle lines are sometimes drawn over the will and power of the board versus the will of the entrepreneur. Without this natural and necessary transition, the potential for abuse of power and misuse of funds, greatly increases. Organizations have folded under the pressure.

On the other hand, entrepreneurs who see the potential *legacy* for their vision early on, will foster this transition. Rather than trying to maintain their authority and power for personal gain or personal gratification, and risking that everything they worked for could be lost, these visionaries allow the organization to grow beyond them.

Collaborative model: This is the last governance power model, which I see the least, but serves as the MOST PRODUCTIVE and lasting. This is where the board and the CEO work as real partners. All the secretive and adversarial overtones are eliminated, and the organization is truly run collaboratively. The only time the CEO is counted out of the picture is when the board is making decisions about the CEO's future. Even then, if you have the right person, this can all be done above board. It's amazing to see a high quality collaborative relationship between a CEO and a board. And this, to me, requires exceptional board functioning. The whole purpose of this book is to provide the kind of understanding to all parties so that they can achieve this Collaborative model. With this in place, the creativity and forward momentum that flow naturally from it, lead to the most successful organizations.

Clearing the Jurisdictional Jungle

So how do you clear away the Jurisdictional Jungle and develop a Collaborative model of governance? Start from the basics. Begin with the bylaws. Do you have a set of bylaws that govern the board's functioning? Have you seen them in the last few years? Have they been reviewed and updated within the past five years? If the answer to any of these questions is "No," chances are you have a case of "Bygone Bylaws." In all my years reviewing bylaws, I am amazed at the number of organizations operating on the kind of "Bygone Bylaws" I mentioned at the beginning of this book. Many I've seen were written 20 years ago or longer. I don't review them from a legal perspective because I'm not an attorney, but I look at them from a logical, governance perspective. And while an attorney should *also* look at them (to make sure they comply with the latest legal requirements for 501 (c)(3) organizations), bylaws should serve an expanded purpose as well.

The bylaws should contain all the corporate information required by State and Federal law, and the usual and customary elements, including general organizational information and purpose, board membership, officers, committees, meetings, approving the annual budget, voting, and requirements for amending the bylaws. In addition, this is a perfect place to establish the requirement for a nine-to-15-member board, as well as outlining the *expectations* of attendance and the process for dismissing board members who do not comply with attendance requirements.

How Often to Meet

The bylaws should include the minimum number of times the board meets each year. As I mentioned, I believe meetings should be held every other month, plus an annual meeting, for a total of seven regular meetings a year. Emergency meetings to deal with sudden issues critical to the organization would be held outside of the regular schedule. The bylaws should also delineate the number of board members who must be present, in order to constitute a "quorum."

Boards that meet less frequently lend themselves to becoming a more CEO-Centered power structure. Boards that meet more frequently, lend themselves to becoming a board-centered or chair-centered power structure. Boards that meet seven times a year, tend to be the most productive boards. It also forces the organization to create a very efficient board meeting, because you have to get a lot done. If you're going to err in this area, I prefer that you choose to meet *more* often, rather than less, no matter how efficient the organization is.

Board members should expect to serve on at least one Board Committee, in addition to attending regular Board meetings. A lot of very important work can be done in committees, and it is a wonderful place to develop leadership.

A paragraph in the bylaws is also needed, requiring directors to attend **all** scheduled meetings of the full board, as a sign of commitment to the important role they have agreed to perform. One unexcused absence per year is allowed and the Board Chair shall have the power to approve an additional absence when notified prior to the board meeting. Board members who cannot fulfill the attendance requirements should be expected to relinquish their position on the board of directors.

The bylaws serve two major purposes, one is to legally guide the board's behavior, but the bylaws also serve as a recruiting tool. When you're bringing a new board member in and they see the expectation for attending meetings, they can honestly decide if they're ready to commit to all the requirements. There are no surprises if it's written in the bylaws.

Boards I deal with are often worried that if they mention mandatory attendance, they'll lose all their members! But if it's in the bylaws, they come onto the board knowing they are expected to be at those meetings.

Other boards have asked me what to do about logistics problems. There are many ways to conduct meetings and with some of the new technologies available, you can now teleconference if necessary. The key is physical involvement -- on site or off site -- seven times a year if you really want to move your organization where it needs to go. I feel very strongly about that.

Even with these elements in place, there are *additional* powers and responsibilities that should be outlined in the bylaws to insure that the board lives up to the increasing responsibilities so crucial to efficient governance today. They include:

1. Establishing, updating and maintaining a commitment to the mission, vision and values of the organization.

The purpose of the board is to establish the broad future thinking of the organization. The Board is responsible for defining the organization's mission, creating a clear, concise vision, and outlining their guiding beliefs and values. The target community served by them should also be identified, and the purpose of their existence should be clearly stated.

When these are required by the bylaws, board directors understand more clearly their roles as the creators and guardians of the organization's mission, vision and values. And it becomes part of their job to regularly (every three-to-five years) reevaluate them in order to keep the organization and its concerns current, vital and successful.

2. Establishing the long-range plan for the organization.

The Board is responsible, in cooperation with management, to create and periodically reevaluate, a long-range strategic plan, and to monitor its success on a regular basis. This may very well be collaboration at its best, as it involves the board, the CEO *and* senior management. It is ultimately a product of the board and can be done on whatever incremental basis the organization desires (three-year, five-year, etc.).

This is actually one of the board's most important duties. I think this needs to be included in the bylaws because I have encountered plenty of organizations that are just now beginning to put together strategic plans. They've had plans in the past that originated from management and were simply endorsed by the board. Many boards don't realize that they are responsible for making sure a long-range plan is created, so they must get directly involved.

3. Setting and monitoring broad organizational policies and approving appropriate operating policies for the organization.

It is the board's job to create the broad overriding policies for the organization. These relate to how the organization is going to operate on a *broad* scale, versus the day-to-day operating policies, which are established by management. The purpose of these policies is to define what needs to be accomplished -- the critical, measurable outcomes and broad processes that will direct the organization and the board along a desired course. Policies should convey, by their nature, a logical rationale for their existence.

Organizations that have a clear mission, vision and values can operate on fewer policies. Too many policies create a cumbersome and all-too-often counterproductive situation, and can create an adversarial condition between management and the board. When there are too many policies, management may strive to *appear* as if they are following policies, merely to keep the board off their back.

Some policies direct board actions (which we'll address in a minute), and others direct the **organization**.

An "outcome" type of policy is best written in measurable terms. These can define the percent of services an organization will provide to different groups of people. For example, a nursing home board may set a policy that at least 35% of their beds must be occupied by people who qualify for public assistance.

Human Resource Policies

Many organizational policies relate to human resources (HR). While some are board-initiated, most are developed by HR professionals in the organization, in direct cooperation with the board's HR Committee, and are subsequently approved by the whole board. These will include policies covering compensation, paid vacations, paid time off, holidays, affirmative action, severance, dealing with harassment, nepotism and workplace violence.

119

Corporate Compliance

These policies would relate to insuring that the organization operates within all local, state and federal guidelines, and adheres to all laws governing the specific service or industry you are in.

Risk Management

These policies would cover such things as Worker's Compensation, liability insurance, preventive maintenance and OSHA compliance.

Corporate Responsibility

Policies in this category would encompass the organization's community involvement, charitable giving programs, and may include policies requiring local and/or minority businesses to be included in all bids (whenever possible).

4. Authorizing the creation of auxiliary organizations.

These are the auxiliaries, foundations and any other kinds of groups that serve to assist the parent organization in fundraising or carrying out other tasks that the board deems necessary.

5. Maintaining its own effectiveness through the creation and updating of board policies, bylaws, and a Code of Conduct.

This guiding statement should be written into the bylaws to remind the board that part of their job is to improve themselves and create a guiding process so that board members operate efficiently and properly. To direct the board's actions, policies would be established regarding conflicts of interest, travel reimbursement, and anything that is not covered in the bylaws.

6. Creating, maintaining and actively participating in an effective process for board member selection and leadership development

As I described in Dysfunctional Diversity and Turnstile Leadership, a board is only as good as its composition and leadership. Part of a board's responsibility should be to proactively define the qualities they need in new board members. They should actively recruit and educate new board members, encourage new board members to carry on and consistently improve the organization's level of service to the community, and establish a process to cultivate talent and encourage those with appropriate skills to take on leadership roles.

7. Determining the measurable outcomes necessary to evaluate and insure the organization's success.

When boards don't know how to gauge the success of the organization, they often get unnecessarily and inappropriately involved in day-to-day operations. It's one of the biggest problems I run into, and will be discussed in depth under the dysfunction of Minutia Mania. It is up to the board to make sure they get the information they need from management to establish the gauges of success for the organization.

Board bylaws should also contain a statement that says, "The primary duty of a non-profit board is to govern the organization in such a way as to meet the needs of the people being served, respond to the needs of the community-at-large, and govern in accordance with all applicable local, state, and federal laws."

Once again, this guides the board in its appropriate role. The board is responsible for *developing* policy and insuring that it is implemented, but the board itself is not responsible for *executing* that policy.

Since the board employs a CEO to carry out policy, they must also establish proper accountability structures to insure that policies are appropriately implemented. Such structures should include regular financial and outcome reports, created by appropriate staff, and submitted through the CEO or appropriate committees to the board.

8. Selecting, retaining, evaluating, and (if necessary) dismissing the Chief Executive Officer.

This should be written into the bylaws as the job of the board *as a whole*. It must be clearly stated so that it cannot be misinterpreted as the responsibility of *anyone* else -- not the Executive Committee or the Chair.

Bylaws should also have a paragraph defining in general terms what the CEO's job is, and clarifying, in no uncertain terms, that the CEO is accountable to the board as a whole, and not to any individual board member or committee.

For example:

"The Board of Directors shall hire a qualified Chief Executive Officer, who shall be responsible for the overall management of the facilities of the organization. The CEO shall enforce the policies, rules and regulations relative to the level of service and safety of the people we serve, and the protection of their personal and property rights; and plan, organize and direct those responsibilities delegated to him or her from time to time by the Board of Directors. The CEO shall be accountable to the Board as a whole, and not to any individual Board Member or Committee."

This will insure that you get more highly qualified CEOs. I believe very strongly that as CEOs become even more of a valuable commodity in the future, people looking at these positions will be looking at how the board functions, before committing themselves to an organization.

One extremely well-qualified CEO I know said that one of the reasons she wouldn't want to leave the organization was because of the wonderful relationship she had developed with her board. And I think we're going to see more and more of that in the future.

9. Creating, maintaining and supporting an ongoing process for generating charitable gifts and donations, to insure the financial health and growth of the organization.

This should be formally written into the bylaws. I have been in too many situations where boards are surprised to learn they are not only responsible for the oversight of existing funds, but are also responsible for ensuring that sufficient funds are raised for future needs. It needs to be made clear from the very beginning, that it is the responsibility of every board member, and the board of directors as a group, to insure that sufficient money is raised or is available to meet the budgetary expenses of the organization.

Board members should financially support the work of the organization, encourage others to contribute, and actively work to attract the resources that make the organization's programs possible; including identifying and cultivating prospects for solicitation and communicating the needs of the organization to friends, family, associates and members of the community.

By including this in the bylaws, you once again let people know *before* they join the board, that while they don't have to be a major donor, they *will* be involved in actively assuring that the organization has enough money and resources to function successfully.

Remember the important balance between work, wisdom and wealth. If you expect a big check from everyone on your board, the balance becomes skewed. And while I believe every board member needs to be *involved* and concerned with the fundraising process, work can bring in money too. Enough carefully-placed phone calls to potential donors can often bring in more money than any single board member could donate from their own account.

A good example of this involved a young man who was just starting his career. He was very interested in an organization I was working with, and was serving on the board. And while he was not making a lot of money, and would not have been able to write a big check like some of the other board members, he *was* working in the advertising field, and his knowledge of marketing and market research was of tremendous value to the board. In fact, the amount of money the organization *saved* by using this young board member's knowledge, instead of paying for the services of a professional advertising agency, was actually a far **greater** contribution than most of the other board members could donate from their bank accounts! So, no matter how each board member is able to contribute, through their work, their wisdom, or their wealth, they are *still* individually responsible for actively supporting any necessary *additional* fundraising required to keep the organization financially viable.

Bylaws are a legal document and you have the right to create them the way you want. This is amazing legal power the board has over its *own* conduct, as long as all local, state and federal mandates are respected.

The most important step in clearing through the Jurisdictional Jungle is to **clearly define the powers of authority** for all the major entities involved. This includes the CEO and all of the board committees. (The board's authority should be defined in the bylaws).

The Jurisdiction Agreement

A very simple and efficient way to define authority is through the creation of a Jurisdiction Agreement. This is a tool I designed about 20 years ago. It's been one of the most popular tools I've shared, and is simply a one to two-page document that guides decision-making for any entity that has decision-making power *and* answers to the board. Jurisdiction Agreements are separate documents from the bylaws, and I have included a couple samples in Appendix E.

Jurisdiction Agreements have three (3) levels of authority. It is important that these be brief, yet very clear documents. And because they are considered "agreements," the party granting the authority, and the party taking **on** that authority must both agree to them.

The first level of authority is called **"Act and Don't Report."** For anything listed under this category, the individual or group has full authority to make decisions. They do not even have to tell the person or body granting the authority what they've done in these areas. They are expected to make certain decisions and will be held accountable for the results of those decisions.

The next level is **"Act and Report."** For anything listed under this category, the individual or group has full authority to make decisions, but must provide a report to the authority-granting entity within a stated amount of time (e.g. by the next board meeting, once a year, every quarter, etc.).

The last and lowest level of authority, **"Report and Act"** requires that the individual or group get approval or at least clarify what is being planned, and obtain authorization **before** doing it.

The examples will clearly show the differentiation. And in Jurisdiction Agreements with individuals who have ongoing authority, it is also important to include a clause that says, "Anything not stated in this agreement, is considered a 'Report and Act' level of authority, until otherwise redefined."

The power of Jurisdiction Agreements is tremendous. In the appendix, I have included one between the Board of Directors and the Executive Committee, and another Jurisdiction Agreement between an administrator and the board.

Some of the most counterproductive, time-wasting, and critical issues occur when people take authority they **shouldn't** have, or when people *don't* take authority they should have. Frankly, no committee should be allowed to exist without a Jurisdiction Agreement. A clearly defined Jurisdiction Agreement is their guide to what they have to do. Committees that have used them, love them. And if the number one reason people leave boards is that they feel their time is wasted, this is one of the greatest ways to keep people motivated, and spending their time well. They will know what authority they have. And they will feel the power they have to make things happen. Almost all the issues I see between board members and management, are decisions that *should* have been made and weren't, or those that were never clearly defined in the first place.

This is also an outstanding tool to use between managers and any person who reports to them (with decision-making responsibilities). It will literally create the kind of environment where decisions will be made, where they'll be made more effectively, and where they will have greater meaning because people feel a sense of confidence, accountability and respect for the decisions they are expected to make.

When I wrote earlier about bylaws and the essential powers that need to be outlined, I suggested that efficient board function is maintained a number of ways. One of them is through a formalized Code of Conduct. The Code of Conduct outlines expectations and states the rights and responsibilities of each member of the group. This also helps prevent the problems associated with Altruistic Self-Interest, as discussed in Chapter 11.

The guide to creating a Code of Conduct is stating what we normally think is obvious. One of the biggest problems I see, particularly with new board members, are people who don't speak up. They may have a concern or question, but will remain silent because they don't feel they know enough yet, they're too new, or they feel their question may be viewed as foolish.

I also run into situations where people overstep their bounds and talk too much! They just keep rambling and don't leave breathing space for someone else who might want to jump in (if they were given the chance). They simply don't show respect for others, or offer encouragement to those who may have questions. And so while we all *assume* that it's human nature to be courteous and respectful of other people's viewpoints, unfortunately, I don't always see that in boards. I have seen things get so heated, that even the best leader would have trouble squelching the negative interaction. Board members need to agree to a Code of Conduct.

You can use the one in Appendix D as a model, or create your own, but these things do need to be stated. Even the most well-meaning people can get swept up in their own emotions and become a disruptive and ultimately counterproductive force when they have not agreed to adhere to a Code of Conduct. And dealing with disruptive people is one of the biggest complaints and concerns leaders express in my workshops around the country.

The Code of Conduct also gives the chair (or whoever is in charge of the meeting) the power to *remind* people of their agreement when they become disruptive, or in some way impede the proper flow of the meeting. Board Member Rights & Responsibilities also reminds the **chair** that they have a *responsibility* to help maintain the rights of everyone, and to keep them on track regarding their responsibilities.

13

Misguided Meetings

Ineffective meetings are the number one time waster for boards. Board and committee meetings are the major means by which boards do their jobs. Yet meetings are probably the most neglected aspects of improving board productivity.

In a nutshell, here are the main causes of what I refer to as "Misguided Meetings":

1. A lack of, or an ineffective agenda

I am amazed at the number of committee and informal board meetings (not necessarily the *formal* board meeting) where no agenda is created.

2. Unclear meeting purpose

How many times have you left a meeting, scratching your head and wondering why you even met?

3. Interpersonal conflict

When you bring people together for very important issues and purposes, conflict is more apt to occur.

4. Ineffective meeting leadership

Go back to the concept of Turnstile Leadership (Chapter 10). Ineffective leadership not only affects the success of meetings, it affects the future of the board and the organization.

5. Intermittent attendance

I'm harkening back to the Bigger is Better syndrome (Chapter 8) and my call for mandatory attendance. One of the most exasperating and amazing phenomena are boards that do *not* expect people to be at meetings! And then they're surprised when good people leave!? Way too much time is wasted helping people who didn't come to the previous meeting "catch up." And even **more** time is wasted when decisions made at one meeting, are changed at another, because different people attended the second meeting! And beyond wasting time, it also drives well-intentioned people crazy!

Let's look at each of these causes of Misguided Meetings individually.

Lack of, or Ineffective Agendas

Just having an agenda, while it is a positive step, is not enough. The quality and design of the agenda is essential to the success of any meeting. The reason an agenda is important, and the way it benefits the physical process of meeting, is that it focuses group energy. It is designed to give people a roadmap for staying on track.

Agendas enable people to better prepare for a meeting. It lets them know what they need to know, or what they need to find out prior to the meeting, in order to be an active and productive participant. When designed properly, agendas assure more efficient use of time. The power of factions and personal agendas is severely limited when the leader follows a written document and keeps the group on track.

Even a less forceful leader can guide detractors back to the topic simply by saying, "We've agreed to this agenda. Let's stick with the agenda." It actually serves leaders who are less dynamic, and keeps the group heading in the right direction.

A well-written agenda also fosters a greater sense of individual and group accomplishment. The best gauge of a successful meeting is when people leave feeling their time was well spent. If the agenda is accomplished, people are more apt to feel that a successful meeting has occurred, and this is a great motivator for volunteers to continue their efforts and involvement.

Guidelines for Creating Effective Agendas:

Agendas should be brief and clearly written in a standardized format. One of the biggest mistakes groups make in meeting planning is to *assume* that they can cover more topics and information than they actually have time for. When designing an agenda, honestly consider how much you can accomplish, knowing the nature of the group and the discussion that will most likely occur. Most experts believe that two hours is optimum, the most any group can endure in one sitting, and still stay productive. So, if board meetings need to go longer than two hours, schedule a sizable break between every two-hour segment. If you're planning a four-hour session or board retreat, schedule a 30-minute break in between for people to regenerate, socialize and so on. Design your agenda with that concept in mind.

Agendas should be written clearly enough for people to understand easily what is planned. The more standardized you make the format of your agenda, the more successful you will be. People should be able to determine exactly how the agenda flows, every time. Choosing a "boilerplate" approach with different information in it every time, is better than allowing agendas to be done differently from meeting to meeting. A different style of agenda creates a need for people to rethink the way they gain the information from that agenda. A standardized format does not.

"Consent agendas" are a great idea as a section of the full agenda. These are a number of items, designated for "consent" only, and put on the agenda to be approved as a group. It might be routine information, like the minutes of the last meeting, or a list of people who've been named to different committees. All of the items on the consent agenda are approved simultaneously, with one vote. Also included on the consent agenda will be any items or issues that have already been discussed and where a plan of action has already been established. All the support materials have been laid out, so the basic understanding is, "These are ready for our endorsement. Unless you have a concern **ahead of time**, nothing on the consent agenda will be discussed at the meeting. We are ready now to approve the xyz project." There's no filibustering or debate at the meeting. If there are any nagging concerns about items listed on the "consent agenda," board members must present their concerns to those in charge *before* the actual meeting takes place, and a single consent item may be removed from the consent agenda.

Agendas should be brief. The shorter they are, the better. And participants should get a copy of the agenda at least three days -- and no more than a week -- prior to the meeting. If you send it out too soon, people don't look at it. They aren't yet *tuned* to thinking about the meeting, so they may set the agenda aside or lose it, and end up coming to the meeting *less* prepared. The same is true if you send it out too *close* to the actual meeting. That doesn't give people sufficient time to prepare. I've seen organizations, in an attempt to look efficient, send an agenda out three weeks before the meeting! But I've also seen agendas handed out *at* the actual meeting. Both practices can cause problems.

The agenda should state the purpose of the meeting as completely as possible, or the purposes of each section of the meeting. For example, a purpose might be to "decide" on how much money to allocate for some project.

All "new business" agenda items should be noted in priority order so that if there is any problem with timing at the meeting, the most important issues are addressed **first**. That way, when people leave the meeting, even if they feel they haven't accomplished *everything* on the agenda, they know that the most significant organizational issues were completed.

Anticipate and assign a specific time frame to **every item**. Without timeframes, there are no expectations, discussions can run on, and by the end of the meeting, the feeling of failure and "wasted time" occurs. An established timeframe encourages efficiency among people as they deal with any given section of the agenda.

Any materials people will need to bring to the meeting should be listed **right on the agenda**. I know you're dealing with adults, but it is a sign of respect to let people know that they will need to bring (for example) their board minutes from the last meeting, a specific report you will be discussing, or the bylaws. Don't assume people know what to bring. Whatever is needed, put it on the agenda. Without the proper materials, some people will come unprepared, and feel lost. Discussion can be bogged down, and time will be wasted.

Also listed on the agenda, whenever possible, should be any pre-assigned responsibilities. For example, "Jackie Johnson will bring information on the cost to rent a bus for the week."

On the bottom of the agenda, print the name AND PHONE NUMBER of the person who is responsible for any agenda changes. So often, organizations assume everyone knows the phone number of the board contact person. Be good to your volunteers. Don't force board members to look up phone numbers. If you need people to *respond* to the agenda, deal with consent items, or make changes, identify the phone number, e-mail address or any other appropriate and efficient way to contact your board connection. Put it right on the agenda.

Limit all of the above information to one printed page, and attach any needed support materials. I believe that one page covers about two hours. If you go beyond one page, there's a very good chance you will not accomplish all you're setting out to do, and people may leave, feeling their time was wasted. When you bite off just about exactly what you can chew, you insure that people are energized to come to the next meeting. Assuming you can do more and cover more than most people can, is arrogant, disrespectful to your board members, and sets you up for disappointment. It is simply a very bad, counterproductive practice.

Wherever possible, within your agenda, list the "type of interaction" for each agenda item, whether it will be something to debate, decide, discuss, inform, clarify, create, or develop. I've included a sample agenda in Appendix F. This kind of information affects how people are prepared, and how they use time.

Types of Interactions:

Debate:

If you have an item on the agenda that you know is going to be contentious, there's a good chance it's going to be a debate and people will take sides. So, by putting the word "debate" on your agenda, it lets people know that time is being allotted for people to argue in a constructive, respectful manner. If you don't specify "debate," and people expect something else, but *end up* in a debate, it's going to take longer, some people are going to feel cheated because they weren't prepared to debate, and you have now mismanaged their time.

By putting the word "debate" on the agenda, you give people an opportunity to prepare and you set them up for the type of interaction that will transpire. It also helps you set the timeframe, and allows for a continuation to the next meeting if it's determined that it's a bigger issue than originally thought.

Decide:

The word "decide" listed on the agenda, tells board members they should plan to leave with a decision. One of the most powerful problems in meeting effectiveness is when people come prepared to make a decision, prepared to come to a conclusion, and no decision occurs; once again, wasting their time. When people come to an agenda item that requires a decision, but not everyone in the group realizes that's the goal, those who are *not* anticipating that a decision should be made at this point, will often inadvertently sidetrack the entire group. This takes the group away from the decision, and into areas of unnecessary clarification or further debate! Then, what so often happens, is that the allotted time runs out, the item is continued to a future meeting, and the majority who were *ready* to make a decision, often leave feeling profoundly frustrated.

Unless there is a clear indication, right on the agenda, that this is an issue to "decide," people won't necessarily know. As simple as it may seem, merely placing the word "decide" next to the agenda item, lets people know that there is an *expectation* for the discussion to end and for the group to come to a conclusion -- a decision -- that they can agree on. Seeing the word "decide" guides people into making sure they have any material they need *prior* to the meeting, so they are ready to work toward mutual agreement, make an enlightened decision, and achieve real closure on an issue.

One of the biggest complaints I hear in my interviews with board members is that their board and/or committee has a terrible time making decisions. This is a simple, but definite step in remedying that situation, and I will cover it in more detail in the next chapter on the dysfunction of Decision Paralysis. Making these kinds of decisions, and plenty of them, is the obligation of every board member.

Inform:

The word "inform" listed next to an item, means it's the board's job, at that point in the meeting, to simply listen. The information they are about to hear may be coming from a staff member, the CEO, Board chair, a committee chair, or from a committee member. The purpose of an "inform" item may be, for example, to give you the latest information on a federal regulation that will be affecting the organization. "Inform" is an opportunity for you to listen and learn. You will not be expected to talk, discuss or get involved. It's actually a polite way of saying, "Please sit there quietly and listen right now. We need to tell you something important." Just make sure that when you designate "inform," you're not dealing with an interactive agenda item. The "inform" items should be the quickest, and most predictable timewise.

Go ahead and ask a couple of questions if you'd like, but be aware that "inform" items are **not** slated for discussion or clarification. Beware! There are question-askers on almost every board, and they can take the entire meeting off track for an hour, trying to get information they could learn other ways. Think of "inform" as a mandate that tells everyone in essence, "If you have major questions, they are **not** going to be answered at this point."

I have known board members who have come to meetings anticipating they'd be "informed" and the whole thing turns into a two-hour discussion and clarification that gets them nowhere! The people who are asking the questions may feel great, and learn a lot. But 90% of the rest of the board members leave dissatisfied. Those curious question-askers can often learn what they need in background material. If the agenda item is marked "inform," HOLD YOUR QUESTIONS and seek clarification later.

I can't tell you the number of times I've heard board members complain, "Why do we spend all the time on his questions?" No single board member is entitled to hijack the entire meeting. That's why this is an important feature of an agenda and it's something that will really help.

Clarify:

"Clarify" is an opportunity to gain information *and* ask questions. Sometimes, information presented at one meeting may spark so many questions, that a time on the agenda to "clarify" is needed at a subsequent board meeting. More time is allotted to these "clarify" agenda items. More give and take is anticipated. Seeing "clarify" on the agenda encourages people to come prepared to ask questions of an *expert*, and gain clarity on an issue, so that a more enlightened decision can be made in the future.

Create:

To designate an agenda item "create" tells board members they are going to design something from scratch. This could take up an entire meeting! It could be trying to "create" a 10-year vision for the organization. This designation says, "Come with your ideas, and your creative juices flowing! Some decisions may be involved along the way, but we're starting at zero, and we'll hope to be at five or seven or maybe even 10 when we're done!" "Create" is generally the most time-consuming agenda designation (although "debate" comes close). But the idea is, that there's nothing set right now, we're going to get creative and pool our ideas, and we're going to come out with some new direction.

When a "create" agenda item is involved, it is only natural, and should be fully expected, that it may require more than one meeting. The only closure people may feel, is that a piece, or certain percentage of the *creation* is accomplished, depending on the size and complexity of the project. When a "create" item is anticipated, it is sometimes advisable to send it through a committee for preliminary ideas, prior to submitting it to the entire board. "Create" can be used to set criteria for what the organization wants in a new development, or to "create" a new recognition program for outstanding volunteer service. "Create" can be some of the most enjoyable, fulfilling, and time-consuming work a board does together.

Develop:

"Develop" is the concept of taking something that has been created, and producing the steps necessary to make it happen. This designation is most often associated with organizational systems and processes that need to be developed, plans for the future, and policies or documents. You might need to "develop" a statement to give to the press. Once again, it's not something that's already set; it's something that needs to be modified, expanded or improved. It starts with an established idea, but one you have to take further. When you use "create" you're starting from scratch.

The designations of these types of interactions -- debate, decide, inform, clarify, create and develop -- can be added to any agenda, and will *immediately* help your board members understand much more clearly what their involvement will be, and more generally how the meeting time will be used.

The person creating the agenda must examine the purpose of every agenda item, and establish a reasonable timeframe for each. This more conscious approach to meeting time management enables board members to come better prepared and gives them a more clear and realistic expectation for the outcome of any meeting. It's a formula for success. People don't like feeling unprepared at a meeting where decisions are assumed, or surprised by an unanticipated discussion or debate. Those kinds of Misguided Meetings often leave board members feeling confused, upset, and ultimately cheated out of the potential to make their best possible contribution to the organization. Feelings of *successful* contribution are what lead to longevity in peoples' involvement with the organization, and on the board.

Misguided Meetings can make you feel inept and manipulated by the people "in the know." Misguided Meetings are especially hard on new board members, and they're the *last* people you want to disenfranchise. They are the keys to bringing in new blood to the organization, keeping the board alive and vital.

If 90% of the people leaving a meeting feel their time was well spent, the positive repercussions are absolutely immeasurable. Misguided Meetings are powerfully negative, and are clearly the number one flaw of boards and for management groups as well! Think of how many times you've realized that a meeting you were required to attend was a total waste of your time!

Many experts believe about 60% of all meetings are a waste of time! At the board level, we can't afford it. When we meet so seldom, it becomes a necessity to competently manage every meeting.

But with all the skills, knowledge and techniques available to create highly productive meetings, we are still going to be faced with the biggest meeting squelcher of them all -- the problem that can bog down the process of problem-solving like nothing else -- and that's OTHER PEOPLE.

Everything a board does is directly affected by how board members work together. It enhances the success of the organization, or undermines it. There is a natural tendency for people to have problems and conflict, especially when they're dealing with important decisions and issues of great gravity. But boards can, and *must* learn about conflict, how to deal with it, understand the causes of conflict, and the issues around it.

Conflict is not necessarily a bad thing. It can help people learn and develop better ways of working together. But conflict still detracts from the success of meetings when it's not handled well. Conflict is one of the main reasons people feel a meeting wasn't successful.

Four Kinds of Conflict

There are four basic kinds of conflict: Information conflict, Values conflict, Personality conflict and Style conflict.

Information Conflict:

Information conflict occurs every time the documents, notes and knowledge one person has coming into a meeting, differ from anyone else's. This is why coordinating information is so important for a board or any other decision-making body. Having the same information is critical. You avoid this kind of conflict when you tell people, right on the agenda, what to bring to the meeting. And that's why it's important that whatever information you want people to have to prepare them for these meetings, is information they truly *need* and not more than that (or less). Letting people know what information they need to review *before* they come to a meeting makes sure everyone is on the same page, and diminishes information conflict.

Very often what happens now is that board members come to a meeting and immediately start to feel uncomfortable when somebody "in the know" starts talking about information that may not be widely known. Everyone else may also be feeling uninformed and uncomfortable, but won't say anything about it. Their discomfort is the fault of whoever put the meeting together! That person is responsible for making sure everyone has the same information before the meeting convenes. And believe me, people who feel informationally "disconnected" too often, will eventually leave the board.

That's why mentoring programs are so important. When people know they have someone to turn to for information, they are much more comfortable. People who have the same information are not only better connected to the discussion, but make better, more unified decisions. It is important to ask questions, and you not only have the *right* as a board member to be informed, it's actually one of your three **legal** duties.

Values Conflict:

Values conflict is very common within a diverse group. This kind of conflict however, should be embraced and accepted. Even if everyone on the board had exactly the same values, you still wouldn't necessarily have a board that is best serving your organization.

I have worked with boards that get along beautifully because they are passive, amenable people. They often come from the same backgrounds, and naturally share similar values. That works well as long as the organization is served; but real problems can emerge as organizations change and need to reflect a more diverse set of values than those represented by current or long-standing board members.

We can now have four distinct generations of people operating within one organization, and four different sets of generational values being expressed at any given time. They are influenced by each individual's experiences, and the economic and social times in which those values were formed. These include the ideas, standards and beliefs people have about work, relationships, and volunteering time, among other things, and can be a *major* source of conflict between people who have different beliefs. And while it can be very enriching, people will also need to recognize and acknowledge those differences, and learn to tolerate and appreciate what each generation can bring to the table for the ultimate benefit of the organization.

As organizations plan into the future, they must consider these different sets of values, not only in the people they *serve*, but also in the people *providing* that service. Values differences are a big part of what boards face today. Knowledge of these differences can either enrich the organization, or create a major impasse in discussion and decision-making. Values differences must first of all be acknowledged, and values conflict must be resolved in a constructive, tolerant and respectful way.

As I discussed in Chapter 6, on the dysfunction of Foggy Focus, a board needs to have a common sense of purpose in order to be effective. This comes primarily from the mission, vision and values of the organization. When the values, in particular, that a board creates for an organization are well defined, clear and supported *jointly* by all board members, they become an excellent tool for diminishing the effects of conflicting *individual* values. By making important decisions based on *organizational* values, it is easier for board members to set their personal values aside, for the greater good of the organization. Even for committee projects, the creation of clear purpose and objectives can help diminish the potential conflict that can come from differing values within the decision-making group.

Another method for diminishing values conflict on the board is to utilize a process that acknowledges the values of each individual, and through discussion and negotiation, creates a

NEW values statement that addresses those differing values and incorporates much of their fundamental spirit. In creating this new values statement, individuals are expected to relinquish ties with their own personal values for the sake of decision-making on behalf of the organization. This process is sometimes called compromise, but to look at it from a more positive and constructive viewpoint, I prefer the concept of consensus.

Consensus

Consensus is the process whereby a group of people cooperatively arrive at a decision they can all mutually support. Consensus gives you the ability to discuss the issues that are centered around values and come up with a joint premise that incorporates as much of the content of the different values that are voiced, as possible. A mission statement, for example, is often a values statement. A mission statement is a collection of ideas that the board *blends* together in order to create an overriding statement that everyone can share.

When you make a values-based decision, and use the process of consensus, you get buy-in from everyone, which maintains the cohesiveness and mutual respect of the group. When that decision is made by means of a simple *voting* process -- majority rules -- the "losers" (which could potentially represent *almost* half the board) are going to feel frustrated, perhaps angry, disenfranchised from the "winners," and potentially disenfranchised from the organization! I've seen some extremely heated discussions, and heard stories of people becoming almost violent because of values differences that were not effectively acknowledged and bridged in the process. The board can become splintered, and much less productive. The contentious and uncomfortable atmosphere that is set up by this kind of situation is highly dysfunctional for everyone on the board. People must feel that their values have at least been heard and considered. Anything less could be a potential deal-breaker and you stand to lose good board members over it.

Any decision that can't be quantified or done in an objective format should be examined with an eye toward trying to meld values differences into something everyone can buy into, connect with, and ultimately feel a stake in. That's consensus. It creates more unified and lasting decisions. The more we can look at our values and honestly bring them out on the table, learning to appreciate the differences, the better off the organization will be.

It is important to point out that striving for consensus on values issues is certainly more time-consuming than the traditional "majority rules" voting approach. If you are dealing with an organization that has a spiritual, moral or religious foundation, or one where there is a broad diversity of values on the board, the time you invest in creating consensus on values-based decisions, will produce better governance for the organization. It will also lead to a stronger, respectful and more unified board.

Personality Conflict:

Even some of the most mature, well-meaning, highly dedicated, and intelligent board members sometimes just can't get along! They come to board meetings and *force* themselves to be tolerant toward each other. It's not respectful. And when I conduct interviews with individuals, comments some board members make about each other are mutually derogatory. But it's part of human nature. We do tend to feel an aversion for some people. We may attribute it to "Personality conflict." We just don't mix. Some of it might be a values difference. Some of it might be negative personal experiences we've had with that person, a member of their family, or sometimes with the company they work for! But the problem with the concept of personality conflict is that it's an easy excuse for a quick write-off. You'll hear people say, "I'm sorry, but I just can't get along with that person. I don't like them. I don't respect them. And we're just not going to be able to work together." That kind of dismissive thinking is highly dysfunctional for the board and can undermine the success of the organization.

I'm not saying everyone needs to *love* everyone else on the board, but there must be enough respect among all board members to listen to each other, believe that each person has something valuable to say, and be willing to work together for

143

positive common outcomes and common decisions. That's why I focus my board development work on helping people come to grips with their differences, and learn greater tolerance, appreciation and respect for each other. The greater good of the organization supersedes everything else. "Irreconcilable differences" between board members is disruptive, dysfunctional and unacceptable.

Style Conflict:

In my 25 years of working with boards and people at all levels throughout the organization, I have come to believe that over half of all interpersonal conflict centers around differences in our *behavioral* styles, rather than our personalities. These are not differences in *who* we are, or differences in our deepest beliefs, but rather differences in the way we *operate,* the way we relate to and behave around each other.

By using a technique to help people become more aware of each other's behavioral differences and increase their understanding, tolerance and acceptance of each other, we are able to overcome what is usually a matter of "Style Conflict."

There are basically four different sets of behavior that differentiate people. I call them the "Boss," the "Buddy," the "Backer" and the "Bailiff." Everyone is a combination of all four, but generally one or two styles will influence our behavior more than the others.

The "Boss"

These are the board members who like to be the "Boss." They are focused on results and tend to be pushy and demanding. They are very good at making tough, strong decisions. They are determined and driven (sometimes like a steamroller), but actually really accomplish a lot. Without these "Boss" type movers and shakers, very little would get done. They are the force that makes things happen. But they do tend to be very blunt and need to be in control. You usually do not have to ask them for their opinions, they're pretty much always out there. And this type of board member is not too concerned about the *feelings* of others.

They are aggressive and forceful, and tend to be impatient. These people are not afraid to take risks, which is sometimes intimidating to people who do not share this style. This is the board member who has trouble admitting mistakes, and tends to try to find someone else to blame. They are also selective listeners -- listening only for what they already believe is true -- and do not display a lot of understanding or tolerance of people who have a different style from theirs.

Other people stereotype the "Boss" style as heartless, crude, brash and rough. And for those of different styles, this strong aggressive approach can be irritating and intimidating. But the truth is, these can be some of the most caring people on boards across this country. Their behavior may be tough, harsh, fast and intimidating, but they can have a heart of gold. The "Boss" type of board member contributes a sense of direction and drive, essential to achieving results and keeping a group on task.

The "Buddy"

These are the friendly board members, the people who want you to like them. Relationships are the most important thing to them. They like to be connected and love teams! The "Buddy" type board members are impulsive, interactive and warm. They are light-hearted and smile a lot. They like to use humor (sometimes to a fault), but these people are gregarious, and keep everyone motivated. They are the cheerleaders and optimists on your board.

Where a "Buddy" has problems, is in managing time. They are the outgoing ones, so it's easy for them to lose track of time if they are relating to someone (and they like to talk a lot!). They may think out loud and process out loud. These are the board members who can be on one side of an issue at the beginning of a meeting, and totally switch sides by the end. They do have a tendency to be time wasters and monopolizers. They will share more than you ever wanted to hear! They can be very persuasive, and can see the big picture, but they don't like a lot of details. And because the "Buddy" style is so active and easily distracted, they tend to be the worst listeners of all four different styles.

Other people stereotype the "Buddy" as frivolous people who can't get down to business. And for those of different styles, the monopolizing, socializing, light approach of the "Buddy" can be irritating. But the reality is that these people, as board members, can be very conscientious and very dedicated. The "Buddy" type of board member contributes a passion for ideas, an ability to make things more positive and enjoyable; and their sensitivity to relationships enables them to orchestrate teamwork and keep people motivated -- essential to accomplishing the work of the board.

The "Backer"

These are the board members who make the world go round. When you have a "Backer" style person on the board, you know the job will get done. You tell these people what to do, and they're fully prepared to sit down, do the job, and not stop until it's done. They are hard working and they love it! What makes the "Backer" feel successful is, "mission accomplished." They are dependable, connected and work well with others. They are calm themselves, have a calming influence on others, and are very accepting people. These board members enjoy planning and their focus is process, step-by-step process. Subsequently, they are great listeners, and it's through their listening ability that they validate other people and build tremendous trust. They are not easily discouraged, but they do shut down if circumstances turn chaotic.

This style of person does not really like disagreements or arguments. However, while they may appear amiable and accommodating on the outside, the "Backer" style does keep a sort of file cabinet in their brain, carefully cataloging people's transgressions against them. So needless to say, it is the "Backer" who is most prone to stress. They can be passive-aggressive and will lose their cool now and then, emptying their mental file cabinet. They don't always speak up at meetings, even if they have the best idea in the group. The "Backer" needs to be encouraged by the board leader, to share their ideas and opinions, or they will keep their ideas to themselves, and the group will not be able to benefit from them.

Other people stereotype the "Backer" as wimpy, just sitting and waiting to be told what to do. And for those of different styles, this non-assertive approach can be frustrating. In reality, many great leaders are "Backer" style people because of their ability to build trust. The "Backer" type of board member contributes the knowledge, ability and willingness to get the job done.

The "Bailiff"

These are the board members who, like their court counterparts, handle all the details. They are the cerebral, analytical, details and data people. They keep board members on the straight and narrow, follow the rules, have high standards, and maintain all the important information and necessary numbers. The "Bailiff" is focused on quality. They are cautious and serious, and they have a strong need to keep everything accurate (even to the point of correcting others). This tends to bog the board down, looking at the minutia rather than the bigger picture. They are expert questioners and need to see logic in everything. They cannot accept the notion of, "Don't worry... just trust me."

Private, quiet and attentive, the "Bailiff" is another style where, if they are not drawn out by board leadership, may just leave quietly, taking all of their valuable ideas with them.

Other people stereotype the "Bailiff" as uncreative because they're so cerebral and detail-oriented. And for those of different styles, this exacting, questioning approach can be annoying and time-consuming. But the outcomes you'll get, from the hands and minds of the "Bailiff" can be amazing. The "Bailiff" type of board member contributes quality, thoroughness and high standards, essential to the success of the board and the organization.

147

Overcoming Style Conflict

The primary reason we concern ourselves with understanding peoples' styles, is to encourage an *appreciation* of what everyone has to offer, and a realization that every style makes a valuable contribution. People often mistakenly assume it's personal. They assume people are behaving in ways to intentionally irritate them, and then naturally have trouble working together. When board members come to understand that this is just how a person behaves, and that it's *not* personal, they can then take it a step further. People who learn to appreciate the value of all styles -- even those that tend to be most opposite of their own -- are much more successful at interpersonal relationships. Recognizing your own style and the strengths and irritations it presents, and knowing how to "flex" your style to make people of other styles more comfortable, is the solution to reducing style conflict and bridging major gaps between members of the board.

The success of the board is a matter of interdependence and mutual respect. All four styles, when properly orchestrated, create a highly effective team or work group. And particularly as a leader, knowing how to help people feel style comfort is a powerful skill, and critical information to understand. The less people feel pushed out of their style, the less stress they will experience, and the more compatible people can be with each other. This enables them to work in a much more respectful, cohesive and appreciative manner with everyone.

There are instruments and profiles available to help people determine what their predominant style is, get a better sense and appreciation for the styles of other people, and work more productively with those people. I absolutely recommend that every board, if they want to be truly successful, find some way for their people to do this kind of a self-assessment. It can be a very enriching, very **enjoyable** process for everyone.

The "Boss" tells us what to do, the "Buddy" encourages us to do it, the "Backer" gets the job done, and the "Bailiff" makes sure that the job is done right! Every style is needed, and when it all boils down, what every board member must keep in mind is that everyone is there for the good of the organization. Individual differences must be overcome for the sake of the thousands or millions of people who stand to benefit from the collective decisions you make. Petty human foibles cannot be allowed to jeopardize the work of the board. It is too important a job. Lives may be at stake.

Board members sometimes forget the numbers of people affected by their every decision. These are decisions that affect many, many lives -- decisions that affect whether people receive needed services, and how those services are administered. These decisions affect whether employees feel good about what they do or not. And if you can impress that upon new board members, you have done a major service for the success of the organization. Everyone should go home after a board meeting feeling proud and thinking, "Wow! I did something truly valuable for society today, volunteering my time to make the important decisions that help this organization run well and serve this community."

Peer-to-Peer Evaluation:

One of the ways to diminish the potential for interpersonal conflict that can impede the progress of a board is to create a peer-to-peer evaluation process, where the board periodically looks at itself. I know what you're thinking, "Oh boy... this is dangerous." But it is only dangerous if it's forced on the board. It is not dangerous if the board agrees to do it, perhaps on an annual basis.

Take a look at the example I've put in Appendix G. It is designed to help people remember that their main purpose is to be effective as a group; and not to be disrespectful in terms of time (not attending meetings, or unnecessarily monopolizing meeting time). This is a periodic *reminder* that their main purpose is to make that board a competent, productive group of people who can advance the success of the organization.

This feedback system is designed for each board member to evaluate every other board member. It's done **anonymously**.

So, if you have a nine-member board, you would be responsible for *writing* an individual evaluation of each of your fellow board members; and you would *receive* eight evaluations back, one from each of the other board members who evaluated you. There are any number of ways to pass the evaluation to the person, but one idea is to create individual envelopes, each bearing one board member's name. Then, as each individual envelope is passed around, you slip your evaluation of that person into his or her envelope. Every person's evaluation of Mike Smith, goes into the corresponding "Mike Smith" envelope, and he ends up with eight single sheets of paper. That's just one way to do it. The only stipulation is that process must remain anonymous.

Now, armed with the evaluation results from all your peers, you must then decide how you want to *react* to the feedback you've just received. Remember, when you agree to employ a feedback system like this -- a process accepted by everyone, created with a set of standards designed to help the board function better as a respectful, unified body -- you are also in essence agreeing to be *open*. You are agreeing to the kind of honest give-and-take that will help everyone make personal changes for the greater good of the group and the ultimate success of the organization.

What I have discovered in my years of using these feedback evaluations, is that when a board member receives eight other evaluations saying they tend to monopolize, that board member becomes self-conscious enough to make an effort not to monopolize in subsequent board meetings. Mutually agreed-upon feedback that is fair, anonymous, and distributed equally to all board members, eliminates the defensiveness that could be brought on by any open confrontation, and helps them to thoughtfully consider and be more open to the opinions of their peers.

I have never seen this feedback process cause anyone to resign. The decision to do it in the first place is a joint decision. You can't push it on your board. Neither the chair nor the CEO can push this. Just by virtue of merely *seeing* the instrument --

without actually *doing* it -- one group I worked with changed their behavior and quickly became much more cooperative. People often *know* what they're doing is counterproductive, and just seeing the expectations laid out in the evaluation form can spur them on to change.

This is part of the balance between advocacy and accord that I mentioned in Chapter 11 on Altruistic Self-Interest. Accord is essential to the decision-making process, especially when it comes to important decisions that must have strong board support. Evaluations are also important to keep individuals growing and developing, and to keep the board functioning at its highest level.

14

Decision Paralysis

Any dysfunction in the board's decision-making ability can be a **major** roadblock to the success of the organization, since one of the three functions of governance is to make decisions! (Remember: defining, deciding and evaluating). And although boards that work well together and get along no doubt feel *good* about what they do, they may actually be making very *few* decisions! Some boards take the easier (and dysfunctional) path of merely *endorsing* decisions made by other entities (like the chair or Executive Committee). While these may be very cordial boards, they honestly aren't doing their job! Some aren't even sure when they're expected to make a decision! And while the agenda form that I mentioned and the other techniques for more effective meetings help with that, there is still more to it.

While roadblocks to effective decision-making have been uncovered in some of the other dysfunctions outlined previously in this book, this is such an important issue, that at the risk of being somewhat redundant, I'd like to take this opportunity to focus on it briefly as a separate dysfunction.

The main causes of Decision Paralysis are:

1. Ineffective meetings
   (already examined in Chapter 13, "Misguided Meetings")
2. Faulty leadership
   (already examined in Chapter 10, "Turnstile Leadership")
3. **Impaired information**
4. **Lack of business acumen**
5. **A board "caste system"**

Ineffective meetings and faulty leadership are certainly at the top of the list, and cause so much Decision Paralysis that they have been covered in their own chapters! But those are not the only causes of Decision Paralysis, and it's not enough to solve those problems without addressing these additional causes.

Impaired Information

With too much, too little, or inappropriate information, boards can't make good decisions. Information management is the key. Boards that want *too much* information (more than they need), tie up staff time. That ultimately costs the organization. Boards that allow the CEO and organizational leadership to determine the information the board needs, can end up with information that is unnecessary, insufficient or superficial. Then, when there's an organizational problem, where the board should have been better informed, everyone looks bad and the "blame game" often begins. Information management needs to be a joint effort. It is the board's responsibility to *tell* management what they need, and management's responsibility to work in a close, cooperative way to insure that they get it. The board needs to sit down with management and discuss the kind of information they need, how it is best distributed, and when they want it. It is **inappropriate** for the CEO and management to determine what information the board should and shouldn't receive. When the board and management are not working as a team, Decision Paralysis is inevitable. An open line of communication must exist between the board and the organization's leadership, where there is an ongoing discussion of what information is needed, and how it is best communicated to board members.

Take the organization's financial report, for example. It is probably one of the most important reports a board can get, but the way it is traditionally presented, some members of a diverse board may not understand it. These reports are traditionally written in a financial language that is not commonly understood by people who have limited experience in the world of finance and accounting. It is therefore the job of the CEO, the board chair, and whatever committee may be involved (in this case, the Finance Committee) to be sure information is clarified. Take your thinking back to square one. If board members don't understand something, they cannot make effective decisions. Financial reports, and all other reports for that matter, need to be created in a way so that every board member has a solid understanding of what they're seeing. Budget decisions, and decisions about the oversight and stewardship of every other area of the organization **depend** on clear communication.

New board members may choose *not* to ask for clarification, for fear they will look foolish or appear uninformed (like the story of the King's New Clothes). In *not* pursuing the information they need, they are actually shirking a legal responsibility. "Duty of Care" requires diligent, attentive and **informed** participation. That is one of the main reasons all board materials should be written so that everyone can understand what is being communicated. And it is up to each board member to require that, and do what they can to create a process for clear communication. Some boards I have worked with have created an Information Management Committee. The purpose of the committee is to work with management, determining the kinds of information needed by the board and its committees, the best ways to present that information, and how often it needs to be produced. If you're like some of my clients who bristle at the thought of having a new committee, this function can be added to the duties of an existing committee. One organization added this to the functions of their Executive Committee.

Lack of Business Acumen

Board members also need to know the *basics* of the business or industry their organization is involved in. Basic business acumen is critical to the ability to make good governing decisions on behalf of the organization. Learning about the organization through the minutes of the last few meetings, or from brief information sheets designed to prepare people for an upcoming meeting, is not enough. Remember, people may be coming onto the board from any number of areas within the community. They may have been recruited through religious, sports, school or other civic affiliations. And while they are dedicated and ready to be board members, desire is not enough. It is up to the management of the organization and the leadership of the board to make sure current and prospective board members are *regularly* informed in the basics of the organization's business.

Some organizations dedicate a certain amount of board meeting time to educating the board on the latest trends in the industry and the latest information on the services they provide. ALL boards should be privy to this kind of information. Touring the facilities periodically can also help optimize their knowledge and give them a stronger "feel" for and dedication to the organization and the people they serve. This knowledge and experience serve as an important foundation for each of them, affecting every decision they make. And as we mentioned in Chapter 6, general board orientation, beyond a building tour, is another opportunity to improve the business acumen of new board members.

A Board "Caste System"

When people have been on a board for a long time, and are comfortable making decisions together, a kind of "caste system" often emerges. Elite "insiders" sometimes even talk in shorthand! Other people on the board, particularly newer board members, are often made to feel like outsiders. This kind of board division can spawn all kinds of Decision Paralysis. Those who have been on the board a while sometimes hold on to their knowledge and experiences, in an effort to maintain a sort of "mystique." This can cause an interrupted flow of information that is critical to effective decision-making for the whole body.

As we discussed in an earlier chapter, mentoring programs can help this situation tremendously. New people can effectively stonewall a decision until they have a greater knowledge of what's going on. They have the responsibility to be informed! A kind of battle can be waged between the long-timers and the newcomers. But if each new board member is mentored, it is a brilliant opportunity for information to be shared. Information is the number one tool of a board's success. Nothing can alleviate Decision Paralysis like clear, concise, appropriate, accurate and timely information.

15

Minutia Mania

The final dysfunction is something I call Minutia Mania, but it's not a small issue! It's really the concept of boards getting involved where they shouldn't, in the day-to-day affairs and internal workings of the organization. It is important to point out, however, that boards can *legally* request as much detailed information as they want. They can delve into any area of the organization's day-to-day operations they feel is necessary. But, if the organization's leadership is doing their job effectively, and the organization is running well, the board should have no need to investigate and involve themselves in Minutia Mania. And yet, many boards still cross over the line. It's not that they can't, mind you... it's just that they shouldn't! Boards should strive to procure **exactly** what they need, to make **informed** decisions in the **best interest** of the organization. That's the key. It is absolutely not in the best interest of the organization, nor is it even appropriate, for the board or any *individual* board member to micro-manage, even if it's the board chair!

I have been in situations over the past few years, where the board chair questioned staff members or management over some very vital issue. And while it is sometimes necessary to conduct an inquisition, exactly HOW it is done is very important.

Handling Minutia Mania well is dependent on the board's ability to know what is appropriate and necessary for them to know, and what isn't. They need to know how the board should go about doing things that seem to *overstep* their normal bounds. When the board is out of step on these issues, it can create the impression that management is not trusted. Overstepping and turning into a Minutia Maniac is invasive, disruptive and often inappropriate! And when it gets to the point where management starts to feel threatened and hassled, the organization runs the risk of losing some of it's best leaders. Minutia Mania can drive people crazy... and then ultimately drive them out. And yet, boards do need to strike a balance. It is their responsibility to provide oversight for the organization's functioning and the proper execution of the mission, vision and values. It is their responsibility to assure that organizational resources are managed prudently. Boards I've worked with who suffer from Minutia Mania began their over-involvement as an honest reaction to feelings of concern about the unknown, and worries about potential risks for their organization.

So how can you assure that the board is achieving proper oversight, without getting involved in day-to-day operations? Let's take a look at the main causes, and the solutions to the dysfunction of Minutia Mania.

The Main Causes of Minutia Mania:

1. Lack of clear standards for evaluating the success of the organization
2. Lack of clear standards for evaluating the CEO
3. Too many board meetings
4. Lack of (or ineffective) long-range planning

Lack of Clear Standards for Evaluating the Success of the Organization

When boards have no way to **objectively** determine if their vision for the organization is happening, or if what they defined in the strategic plan is occurring, how can they know that the organization is successful? If they don't have that sense, and instead find themselves feeling "concerned," they tend to plunge right into the heart of Minutia Mania.

Too little time is spent defining the gauges of the organization's success. A board has a right and obligation to know how successful the organization is, and how it will be judged, and exactly how that success is gauged. Beyond the success of the CEO, the board needs to know that the organization is, in fact, achieving what the board wants it to achieve.

Traditionally, financial well-being was the only gauge boards considered, but times have changed and it is no longer enough. It is no longer the best we can do in determining the health and success of the organization. Years ago, doctors had limited methods for determining a person's health, and now have the advantage of access to highly-sophisticated blood testing systems, MRIs, ultrasound and other advanced diagnostic tools. Today's board similarly must go beyond assessing the traditional financial "pulse" of the organization and now create gauges to assess many more areas of organizational success and effectiveness. This is especially true if they want to be able to avoid Minutia Mania and rest comfortably as a board, knowing the organization is being well run by the CEO and management. Gauges need to be created today to assess the achievement of strategic plan initiatives, risk management, customer satisfaction, employee satisfaction, corporate compliance, community stature and service quality. Using these new diagnostic tools, boards will have a much clearer view of an organization's success, and areas where improvements are needed. Each of these gauges can be defined in such a way as to create objective, measurable criteria for the board to assess. One example of a success gauge might be a designated percent of satisfied customers, based on a customer satisfaction survey. It could also be a percentage of improvement the board wants the organization to achieve in the area of employee retention.

Once these gauges have been defined, it then becomes management's responsibility to provide the necessary information and data, to enable the board to determine how well the organization is doing in each of these areas. The frequency of these reports would be based on data availability, and the cost (in staff time or utilization of outside vendors) to produce this information. In some cases, totally new reporting systems need to be developed to provide the information necessary to assess a specific gauge. For example, several organizations I've worked with created assessment tools for judging employee satisfaction, as a result of the board's desire to assess the organization's success in that area.

Lack of Clear Standards for Evaluating the CEO

As part of my work consulting with organizations, I have been called in to help boards deal with a CEO who is faltering. Sometimes the job involves coaching and helping the existing CEO *regain* his or her stature with the board, and sometimes it involves "counseling out" to help the CEO find an organization better matched to his or her skills and talents. This is often followed with counseling the *board* as they begin searching for a new CEO. For most boards, hiring a new CEO is a paralyzing thought. I am amazed at how often I have to begin by working with the board to get a clear, unified definition from them of what a "successful" CEO looks like! Major mistakes are made in this area every day by boards who don't do their homework. I have also seen boards that will conscientiously do their homework, but then don't follow through with their own plan for hiring the right person!

Let's say you have the right CEO. How do you know that he or she is succeeding and achieving what you expect? Very clear expectations should be laid out. And this should be a cooperative effort with the CEO. The CEO should help the board set up the standards and gauges for his or her success.

Evaluating the CEO is a very important board responsibility. Even though many boards allow most of the actual work to be done by the Executive Committee, the board is collectively accountable for the evaluation of the CEO, and is ultimately accountable for the CEO's future with the organization.

This is a job that should *never* be left totally to the Executive Committee.

Evaluating the performance of the CEO is difficult when it is based on the subjective assessments of board members or subjective recommendations made by the Executive Committee. Some boards I've worked with use a "No news, is good news" approach. If the organization is doing financially as well or better than it did a year ago, and nothing negative related to the CEO's performance has occurred (no headlines or headaches/complaints), then the CEO gets a good review. The bottom line is, most boards I've worked with don't do a very thorough evaluation because they don't have a good set of standards for judging the CEO's success. My recommendation to help boards create these standards, is that 70% of the CEO's success should be based on organizational success. That means that if you create the gauges of organizational success that we mentioned, 70% of your evaluation of the CEO would already be done. The other 30% should then be based on leadership effectiveness and board relations. This is the more subjective area, but is also an important part of insuring that you have the right person at the helm. I have included some Guidelines for CEO Evaluation in Appendix H.

Key Characteristics of an Effective CEO

In my experience coaching CEOs toward better performance, and developing more competent leadership in organizations, I have identified several key characteristics common to the most effective CEOs. In addition to a CEO's ability to come through on the organizational goals, these keys can virtually *eliminate* the need for the board to get into the minutia of the CEO's daily activities.

The key characteristics of an effective CEO, as it relates to leadership effectiveness and board relations, are:

1. Knowledge and skill in sound financial management

A CEO doesn't have to be a financial expert, but must know the bottom line. They must have a deep enough understanding of finance to capably work with and manage financial experts, whether it's an accounting firm, or the organization's CFO. A CEO with broad financial knowledge prevents the CFO from gaining too much power and acting like a pseudo-CEO. I must also admit that it concerns me when organizations purposely hire a former CFO or financial expert to *run* an organization. This is often a reflection of the Dollar $ign Delusion dysfunction which was discussed at length earlier in the book. A financial expert may be tremendous with the bottom line, but in my experience, they often lack the more *human* leadership skills, which are essential to the CEO role in today's complex organizations.

2. Consistent, demonstrated follow-through on commitments

Some CEOs have a habit of making impressive but empty commitments to boards. And while their intentions are good, there is no follow-through! I am amazed at how often boards let this pass. If a CEO isn't coming through on commitments to the board, they may also be neglecting commitments elsewhere, and this will eventually come back to haunt you.

It's also important to encourage the CEO to make ONLY those commitments they can honestly fulfill. When CEOs feel pushed by the board, they make commitments out of fear, for the sake of their own survival. The inevitable failures to meet those commitments are often covered up, seriously eroding the trust between the board and the CEO.

3. Ability to communicate clearly and effectively in all forms

No matter how the board receives messages from the CEO, in written, spoken, or electronic form, the message needs to be **clear**. Clear communication to the board means the CEO is also a clear communicator with employees and other stakeholders.

4. Demonstrated good listening skills

Leaders who are poor listeners can be very poor leaders. If you detect that your CEO is not listening well to the board, chances are he or she is also not listening well in other work-related situations, and may be missing information critical to the success and future of the organization.

5. Ability to develop and maintain the trust of senior staff members

Be very leery when all board presentations are made by the CEO, rather than hearing information or receiving occasional reports from senior staff or top level management, those who are more directly involved in the projects or areas being discussed. CEOs who do *not* include their resident experts, and do all the presenting themselves, either don't want to give away any power, or are afraid their staff may make the CEO look bad. In either case, it is not a sign of good leadership. According to some of the latest theories, excellent leaders are those who know how to orchestrate, encourage, motivate and showcase the talent in their organizations.

One of the best ways to determine whether the CEO has positive support from the staff, is to watch the relationship between the CEO and staff members. In board meetings, at organizational functions and in various other work situations, mutual respect and trust between people is clearly visible.

6. Is respected by most of the organization's employees

This can be easily observed in smaller communities, just by meeting employees outside the work setting. You will hear it in comments people make, or see it in employee reactions whenever the CEO speaks. The way the CEO treats employees will give you a good sense of the level of respect they have for each other. When employees whisper information or begin voicing complaints to board members about the CEO, something's wrong. Even though it's inappropriate employee behavior, the board needs to bring it to the attention of the CEO, while maintaining strict confidentiality regarding the employee who made the original comment. These kinds of comments and issues are a sure sign of a leadership problem.

7. Is regarded as a leader in the community

CEOs, especially those leading most human service organizations, must be actively and visibly connected to the community. Dealing with their daily work and heading home is not enough. Community connection is important, and is easy to determine based on their involvement with various civic groups, volunteering, and their visibility at events where the organization has a presence and the board may be attending.

I worked with an organization years ago, where the CEO appeared to be very competent in many areas, but was continually criticized for not being present at important functions that included the organization. These were public events involving all of the community's social service agencies, city-wide business events featuring all of the community's major employers (of which this organization was certainly one), and even celebrations within the organization itself, where all staff members were invited to attend. This CEO believed that anyone could represent the organization at these functions, and delegated that responsibility (to a fault). This eventually led to a very clearly negative image throughout the community of him as a leader, and board members were keenly aware of it as they interacted within various community settings. Being regarded as a leader in the community puts a high-level human face and personality on the organization itself, and this positive impression provides influence for the organization politically and financially.

8. Can make difficult personnel decisions with a minimum of negative impact on employee morale

If the board has to go through tough personnel decisions, like layoffs, salary reductions or changes in benefits, how well does the CEO handle it? And while some decisions may inevitably create some morale issues, the effective CEO is able to minimize the "human" impact.

When a CEO doesn't efficiently handle a problem *early* enough, major issues can occur, including lawsuits charging discrimination or hostile work environment, and threats of unionization. Because issues of this nature usually develop over an extended period of time, it strongly suggests a CEO who is not taking responsibility for recognizing and solving problems early, or one who is not being held accountable. Either way, the effectiveness of the CEO is compromised. If a CEO can't handle difficult personnel issues, they're in the wrong job.

I worked with two organizations in particular where the CEOs allowed problems to develop too far before intervening. The problems centered around employee issues, both of which had began with very clear early warning signals. One situation was a discrimination lawsuit, another was an attempt to unionize. And in one case, letters threatening legal action against the organization had been written to individual board members. By the time each CEO finally addressed these issues, they had already developed to a level of severity that required board intervention.

The role of a CEO is to make decisions that solve personnel issues BEFORE they become a concern for the board. In any case, it is the CEO's responsibility to inform the board anytime it is detected that an employee problem may be deteriorating or heading toward legal action.

There are also some potentially threatening issues that can occur with little or no warning (e.g. family members charging abuse, people taking their negative experiences with the organization to the press, rather than discussing them with staff or management). In these cases, management is often caught off-guard. Consistent, capable leadership minimizes the impact for these kinds of negative events, and an effective CEO keeps the board informed throughout the process of resolving issues of this nature.

9. Demonstrates thorough judgment in important decisions

When the board asks questions about any actions the CEO has taken, or future plans for the organization, the CEO should be able to answer them clearly and decisively. And while once in a while the CEO may have to check a detail or two, it should be evident to the board that there is thorough thinking behind every important decision, and that those decisions follow a clearly-defined vision or plan.

The main reason a CEO is hired, is to make consistent, sound decisions that further the organization's mission, vision and values.

In my work coaching top executives, I have discovered that confidence in the executive is often eroded by a lack of clear reasoning and/or a lack of plan-based decision-making.

10. Keeps the board properly informed on appropriate issues

The board should **never** be surprised. If the CEO knows something that could adversely affect the organization, the board should be informed. Even if it's a direct communication to the chair, who may or may not be able to inform the whole board prior to the next meeting, an attempt must be made to keep the board (or, at the very least, the chair) informed on important organizational issues. The board that is taken by surprise is the result of a CEO who is not living up to his or her responsibilities.

The board must also be carefully schooled in the critical importance of confidentiality. The board should be considered a trusted confidante for the CEO, and each board member must take very seriously their crucial role in maintaining organizational confidentiality.

11. Demonstrates respect and support for all staff members

This is visible in all settings where the CEO is working with staff members. It is enlightening to watch staff members make reports at board meetings. A good leader leads by developing effective relationships, rather than leading autocratically. The latest thinking is that "great" leadership is based on a person's ability to engender respect and connection with his or her staff.

No one can be an expert on everything, and any CEO who acts that way, would concern me. The key to quality leadership is the ability to **hire** the right people, and let *them* be the experts. The CEO needs to know what's going on overall, but it's important for the board to be able to see that the CEO is surrounded with the right people, and is orchestrating all their human talents successfully.

12. Takes responsibility for decisions, even those that don't have a positive outcome

The minute something goes wrong, does the CEO look for someone to blame, or does the buck stop there? I call top level people the "buck-stops." The responsibility and accountability ultimately lie with the people at the top. The buck stops there. People will make mistakes, sometimes even large ones, but effective leadership depends on the ability to **own** those mistakes and to present a solution to the board, or some process for avoiding those mistakes in the future.

No CEO can function without mistakes. I'd be a little worried about one who never had a problem. There may be litigation and all kinds of organizational issues, but the CEOs you need to watch are those who continually *deny* that they even have a problem, or are unable to realistically see the problem for what it is, and subsequently don't plan appropriate changes to avoid problems in the future.

13. Demonstrates a broad working knowledge of all aspects of the organization

These are CEOs who *know* that they can't personally have all the answers, but are resourceful enough to know who does in any given situation! And they come prepared with the necessary expert(s) whenever it's needed.

14. Freely shares the credit for successes with their staff

There is a wonderful humbleness about outstanding leaders. They are eager to share credit -- not to the point of phoniness -- but they just don't need the glory or the spotlight. The satisfaction they feel comes from knowing they chose the right person to make a project successful.

You can see it in the way the CEO behaves. You can tell when it's real, and when it's an act. Just look at the face of the person who's getting the credit, and you'll know if it's real.

Many years ago, I worked with a very talented CEO of a large long-term care organization. He was telling me how excited he was that his organization had just completed building a multi-bed acute care facility on their campus. In our conversation, he expressed how grateful he was to the hundreds of staff members who had sacrificed to make the project a reality. He explained how they had involved themselves in the planning, building, and moving; managing decisions that had to be made, dealing with the daily inconveniences of being "under construction" and all the while, keeping all the residents comfortable with the chaos happening around them. "Do *they* realize what they've accomplished?" I asked. He suggested that he had thanked people individually, but not in any formal setting. The idea then hit him that to truly express his pride, satisfaction and gratitude to everyone, what he really needed was a formal gathering with the board and staff. The resulting event had a huge positive impact that rippled throughout the organization, and is one of my favorite examples of a leader who really knew how to share the credit.

15. Keeps up on major developments and trends, and is well-read

When the board asks the CEO questions about major issues or developments in the organization, or in the industry, the capable CEO will already be aware of them. Once again, it doesn't mean the CEO needs to have *all* the information. Some issues may still be "in the works" or analysis may not be completed on determining how a new development will affect the organization. But it's pretty easy to determine if your CEO looks like a deer caught in the headlights, or is one who is staying on top of things vital to the industry, and staying informed about issues that may affect the organization.

170

An effective CEO stays informed and keeps the board informed as well. The quality of the material presented to the board can be very telling. You know the CEO is well informed when the written materials the board receives are informationally rich, include ideas from the CEO, and demonstrate an awareness of new trends in the industry.

16. Stands up for his or her convictions, yet is open to new ideas

A strong belief in anything they propose, is important to quality leadership, but there must also be an awareness of what has and hasn't worked in the past, and a willingness to learn from every experience. This kind of honest growth and development in the CEO as a leader, advances the potential for future organizational success.

There needs to be a sense of **conviction**, a sense of **direction**, and a sense of **strength** about what they believe. But it must be strength without rigidity. When a board is in a full, collaborative partnership with the CEO, it is not a problem for the CEO to take the lead with the board once in a while. Remember, in those situations, agreeing with the CEO is not a rubber stamp, it's just good governance.

17. Presents problems *always* accompanied by suggested solutions

When you have a CEO who comes to board meetings only spouting problems, *you* have a problem -- and that problem is the CEO. At the very *least*, the CEO should attempt to suggest a solution. The CEO is paid to come up with solutions.

Now that doesn't mean that the first solution presented will be the one the board chooses. It may not be affordable. It may need refinements. But the effective CEO gives the board at least a springboard from which to jump into solving any issue.

Those are the key characteristics of an effective CEO, whose leadership and character will build the kind of trust between the board and the CEO that will diminish the need for the board to get involved with the minutia of the organization, and decrease the dysfunction of Minutia Mania.

That being said, I'd like to return to the last two causes of Minutia Mania: too *many* board meetings and lack of (or ineffective) long-range planning.

Too *Many* Board Meetings

There are boards out there that just *love* to meet. It may be needed, but not usually. It may be more for social reasons. I think it's fine to get together, but I really feel people should socialize *outside* of board meetings -- outside the realm of dealing with organizational business and meeting the important responsibilities of being a board member. The optimum remains six meetings a year, plus one annual meeting, and committee meetings as needed. That's plenty for just about any organization. When a board meets *too* much, it's often because they need to feel useful and want to feel needed. They want something important to do! And when everything appropriate is already being accomplished, they tend to start looking for other areas where they can be involved and helpful, inevitably crossing the line and meddling their way down into the minutia, and it's simply counterproductive for the organization.

A board has a **legal** right to involve itself at *any* level of the organization, at *any* time, if they believe that there is just cause and that the welfare of the organization hangs in the balance. In the majority of cases, when this occurs, it is a sign that the board has either lost confidence in the CEO, or has not established a trust-based relationship in the first place. Unless there is a clear and objective concern about the CEO's competence or integrity, the board should always work cooperatively with the CEO to satisfy their concerns about anything happening within the organization.

When the board's reason for getting involved at the operational level is based on simple curiosity, or a desire to have more control (beyond what is necessary for good governance), and

172

they begin asking questions and requiring input on operational issues (such as purchasing decisions, vendor selections, or landscaping and grounds-keeping details), they have entered the world of Minutia Mania. One board member I met put *herself* on the agenda, to discuss the color of paint that was used in the hallway of an organization! She had read an article on the psychological effects of color. This led to a lengthy discussion with the board and almost ended in a decision that the board should be approving all paint colors before they are used!

Rubber Stamp Phobia

Another reason boards sometimes schedule too many meetings, is as a reaction to "rubber stamp phobia." They have a fear that the CEO is really running everything, and that the more frequently they meet, the more assured they will feel that they are involved in decisions and not merely providing a "stamp of approval." This is caused, once again, by a weak or ineffective relationship between the board and the CEO. When the level of cooperation between the board and the organizational leadership is high, the board will have little or no fear of becoming a rubber stamp.

Some issues that the board immediately approves are not really "rubber stamps," but signs of a good, working relationship between the board and the CEO. If you have an effective CEO, who comes to the board with proposals and recommendations that are well thought-out, that meet the mission, and are of a quality that shows they've been carefully researched and have a high probability of success, then it isn't a rubber stamp. Saying, "Yes. Let's go with it," is just good governance! As long as the **whole** board has been brought into that decision, and it isn't just a decision from the Executive Committee or chair, you're doing well.

Some boards suffer "rubber stamp phobia" for *legitimate* reasons, because there are a number of highly autocratic, yet highly capable CEOs who manage to *manipulate* the board into becoming a rubber stamp for them. In organizations where such CEOs prove to be very successful as organizational leaders, the board may *willingly* take on the rubber stamping role. And while the goals of the organization may, in fact, be getting met, the problem with this is that it creates a complacent board that, in the long run, will not serve the best interests of the organization.

If the autocratic CEO is replaced by a weaker, less competent executive, this complacency can lead to major concerns for the organization's future. Boards must strike that wonderful balance between becoming a "rubber stamp" (because they're not involved *enough*) and becoming *too* involved.

As a board, be careful. Information is power. Be sure you have the right information. When you do, and you're comfortable, your approval of a CEO's recommendation is an endorsement of quality leadership, and that's great! That's exactly what the board should be doing!

Lack of (or Ineffective) Long-Range Planning

The board may have a plan that is clearly written, but one of the common problems I see in strategic plans across the country are organizations that take on TOO MUCH! When the board bites off more than it can chew, they end up going in a lot of different minutia-oriented directions, and experience a lot of failures, mainly because some plans never even get started! A high-quality, long-range plan, usually doesn't project more than three years, but will include a five- or 10-year *vision*. Clear gauges of success are outlined, along with suggestions and plans for proper funding resources and support. This is the kind of plan that keeps a board busy on appropriate things, and out of the day-to-day operations.

Board leadership also needs to make sure that any individual board member who decides to personally go into the organization and start checking up on things, is *reminded* of the appropriate method for dealing with any concerns. They need to bring it to the board, rather than resorting to Minutia Mania.

Minimizing the Minutia

There is so much that a board *should* be doing, what they need to do and are expected to do for the organization, that they should not allow themselves to get bogged down in minute details or they do themselves *and* the organization a great disservice. By selecting the right CEO and maintaining excellent board leadership, a board can maintain the proper focus.

An appropriately-functioning board focuses on:

The mammoth, not the minute. The only "little" things a board is appropriately supposed to spend time on, are the details of the board itself, and improving their own effectiveness.

Destinations, not directions. The board's job is to discuss and plan where they want the organization to be. It is the job of the organizational leadership and the CEO to determine the directions to get there.

Purpose, not process. What is the purpose of the organization? Why do we exist? Mission, Vision, Values. The actual process required to get there and serve that purpose, is the responsibility of the organization's leadership.

Policies, not procedures. And I mean high-level policies that guide the entire organization -- policies that relate to such areas as ethical business practices, diversity, competitive compensation, use of organizational facilities, retirement programs, and inter-agency relations. These should be policies that stem from the mission, vision and values, and are designed to guide the organization in creating operational **policies** and making decisions. Carrying out the day-to-day operational *procedures* should be left to the organization's leadership. And the only procedures the board should be concerned with, are those that relate to the board's own functioning.

Outcomes, not operations. The board determines what the organization ultimately wants to achieve. Far too few boards spend time on defining outcomes. If they did, they would have better gauges for the success of the organization, and the CEO as well.

The noted board authority John Carver said, "The majority of board thinking should be future-focused. The board is responsible for creating the future, not minding the shop."

The Board's Business

Let me just go back, for a moment, to the basic concept I introduced earlier in the book about what boards are actually supposed to be DOING. Your **role** is to serve as a visionary, guardian and link for the greater good, prosperity and future success of the organization. To guide that, the board is principally responsible for **fundraising** and financial development; and for performing and maintaining good **governance** (defining, deciding and evaluating) in primarily these areas: planning, programs, budget & finance, human resources, community relations and marketing, and in information management. A board also needs to have an ongoing involvement in developing and improving itself.

Planning

Planning, or more specifically "big scale" planning, includes strategic, long-range and financial planning. The purpose of planning is to position the organization for a successful future, through a process of anticipating and fostering change.

Programs

In the broadest board sense, this is determining what programs the organization will be involved in and which ones they will no longer support. A good example of that is the current thinking about strategic planning, where organizations take a hard, honest look at what they do well, and the areas where they are less successful. This is especially important from a financial standpoint, where decisions need to be made about what programs the organization can realistically continue to fund.

This is an extremely difficult, but essential question. Even if the organization has been providing some service for 50 years, the board needs to examine whether they should continue doing it for the next 50, or phase it out over the next five years. That's an issue in the "programs" area.

If boards don't get involved in the overall scope of these kinds of programs, funding won't happen. The board's involvement in programming assures that programs will be supported, properly funded and carried out.

With the many national initiatives to improve the quality of service provided by organizations, the board also needs to be involved in helping define, create and foster an organization-wide quality improvement plan.

Budget & Finance

Financial governance involves overseeing the way the organization's resources are used. It involves using all the knowledge and resources necessary to maintain future financial health. Those resources include everything of value -- money and other assets, infrastructure, buildings and land.

Human Resources

The most critical resources to the organization are, of course, the **human** resources. The broad scope of human resource involvement, from the board perspective, involves how people are compensated, how they are trained and treated, and the costs and structure necessary to maintain sufficient expert staffing to carry out the goals of the organization.

Community Relations & Marketing

The board also needs to be involved in a community relations and marketing program, so that the organization has the funds to position itself competitively. Even non-profit, social service organizations have to deal with issues about competition in the marketplace, and that's something boards need to be involved in from a broad perspective.

Effectively positioning our organizations has become more important with increasing competition for charity dollars. In the long-term care industry where I do quite a bit of work, there are a lot of highly competitive new ventures in the areas of independent and assisted living. And the next big market for these organizations, the baby boomers, are more knowledgeable, interested, and **demanding** in their search for high quality, elderly living arrangements. Public relations and marketing must speak to them.

Information Management

Information management is a vital board role. Once again, I would recommend an on-going Information Management Committee to oversee this aspect of the organization. This involves any board-related information that is coming in or going out -- between the board and management certainly, but also between the board and any other entity. Remember the importance of the board's role as a "link."

Board Development

Boards also need to take care of and develop *themselves* on an ongoing basis. Some boards create an actual Board Development Committee, or make it part of the function of the Executive or Membership Committee. For the health and well-being of any board and the organization they serve, improving the board's success as a cooperative and productive entity serves the organization immensely. As I suggested earlier, there is often a sense of guilt that goes with the board authorizing organizational dollars to be spent on themselves, but the education board members receive in these kinds of programs is actually an *investment* in the future of the organization. The reason companies all around the world continue to train and update employees is to keep them sharp, on top of the latest technology, and ultimately help the organization stay more competitive in the marketplace.

The same holds true for a board of directors. There are a host of benefits to **investing** in continuous board development:

1. It assures continuity by training sitting board members in how to actively cultivate a more diverse group of NEW board members who can share their work, wisdom and wealth to improve the overall success of the organization.

2. It fosters quality leadership through training and developing people who are skilled at leading others, rather than succumbing to the ineffective practice of giving everyone a "turn" at being the leader.

3. It keeps the board on a well-guided path by defining, maintaining and updating bylaws and policies that guide board actions.

4. It assures outstanding board performance through regular peer evaluations, annual board development retreats, and the possible use of outside board audits, when warranted.

Conclusion

Creating Your Pearl

In the beginning of this book, I talked about change -- the changing role of boards today, as opposed to what they were expected to do years ago, and the importance of fostering the necessary changes in our organizations to keep them successful in the days and years ahead. My purpose in writing this book was to define and outline some of the more common predicaments a board can find itself in, if it doesn't change with the times. And what I hope my readers will gain from all of this, is first of all an expanded appreciation for the importance of non-profit boards today.

I have served my purpose as the grain of sand in your oyster, and the pearl is now yours to produce. I know for some of you, it's going to feel like I've introduced a whole truckload of sand! But take heart. Taking one small step, then another and another, will help you slowly produce the results you want. And even producing a small pearl is better than letting your board bury its head in the sand.

To all the board **chairs** reading this book, I hope your pearl will be to create a leadership legacy that builds the best possible board you can today; mentors and supports the development of new leaders tomorrow; and establishes and continues a tradition of outstanding leadership -- people who are competent and confident -- to take on this very important role for the future success of the board itself, and the organization.

To the **CEO's**, I hope your pearl will be the ability to build the most effective, cooperative relationship between you and your board. I hope that you will see your board as an ally -- as a collaborative partner in the future of your organization -- and that you will do everything you can to be the best possible organizational leader, and a trusted ally to your board.

To all the **board members**, because I wrote this book more for you than for anyone else, I hope that your pearl will be the realization that you are an equal partner in the success of your board. I hope that you will take a more proactive role in making sure your board is the best it can possibly be. And while this is a much larger task than you may have ever thought, with your talent, skill, commitment to the organization and desire to grow, the pearl is there for all of you to create together.

And if you are someone who has ever thought about being on a board, or if you are a **prospective board member**, and decided to read this book with the idea of learning whether this is for you, then I hope your pearl is a motivation to get involved with a non-profit board -- one you feel a passion for. Your knowledge, commitment and excitement, and your efforts as a board member, can positively affect the lives of millions of people -- people who are counting on you to help.

Appendices

Appendix A

Fostering Dynamic Boards

Examples of Guiding Beliefs

- Collaboration strengthens and improves results.

- Organizational development requires individual change.

- Ongoing assessment is critical for quality.

- A professional has a moral responsibility to improve effectiveness through lifelong learning.

- Shared power benefits all.

- The most meaningful change in people occurs when their hearts, minds, spirits and feet are touched.

- Diversity strengthens.

- Example is a powerful teacher.

- Personal and professional development requires the continuous challenging of our beliefs and practices.

- Services must support the rights, dignity and individual needs of the people served.

- Meaningful change requires risk taking in a supportive environment.

- True leadership requires integrity, compassion, and responsibility.

- Employees who feel cherished and respected by their organization provide the greatest quality of service to their customers.

- Employees who are well trained, encouraged and held accountable produce the best results.

- Effective volunteers are essential to our overall success.

- People work harder and better for and with people they trust and respect.

- A well informed community is essential to effective fundraising and a strong volunteer base.

- People are most generous with their time and money when they feel a personal connection.

Appendix B

Mission, Vision and Values Examples

The following examples were taken from the internet and other sources. Each organization has granted permission for these to be reprinted in this Appendix. These examples demonstrate a diversity of organizations and boards, as well as the style they have used for expressing their Mission, Vision and Values. Each was selected because of their clarity in conveying the organization's identity and purpose.

Pierce County Human Services
Developmental Disabilities Advisory Board
Pierce County, Washington State

Mission

It is the mission of the Pierce County Developmental Disabilities Advisory Board to influence the quality of supports to individuals with developmental disabilities to respect personal choice and diversity, ensure fundamental human rights and optimize individual strengths.

Vision

We envision a future where individuals with developmental disabilities have:
- power and choice in making decisions and directing their lives;
- relationships with people whom they love and care about and who love and care about them;
- recognition for what they can contribute to our community;
- active involvement in the communities where they live;
- opportunities to use all of their strengths and support for their areas of need; and
- opportunities to live healthy, safe, and enjoyable lives.

Values

We believe that:

- holistic approaches to supports and services is vital;
- ideas, priorities, and solutions must be developed at the community level;
- services must be responsive, flexible, and tailored to meet changing needs throughout an individual's life;
- services must be barrier-free and accessible;
- every person in the community can make a contribution;
- every person must be treated with respect, compassion, and dignity;
- diversity enriches our community, and we must build upon this strength;
- each person's unique cultural, spiritual, and developmental needs must be respected;
- responsibility is shared in partnership with the community;
- an attitude of cooperation and collaboration must be demonstrated;
- services must be efficiently operated and proven effective for those served; and
- we are advocates for needed change.

Special Libraries Association
Washington, D.C.

Mission:

To advance the leadership role of our members in putting knowledge to work for the benefit of decision-makers in corporations, government, the professions, and society; to shape the destiny of our information and knowledge-based society.

Vision and Values:

Our vision is to be known as the leading professional association in the information industry - a catalyst in the development of the information economy, and a strategic partner in the emerging information society.

Committed to professional excellence, we value:

- Our clients and our ability to respond to their needs adding value to information services and products
- Continuous learning and professional development
- New paradigms of information service and delivery, and the opportunities they provide for our continued role in the information economy
- The use of technology to enhance our jobs, our organizations, and society
- Opportunities for networking - for us to meet, communicate, and collaborate
- The leadership role of the Special Libraries Association
- The Association's efforts to help us strengthen our roles as information leaders in our organizations and in our communities
- The role of the Association in the development of information policies

Hopewell Valley Regional School District
Pennington, New Jersey

Mission Statement

The mission of the Hopewell Valley Regional School District, in partnership with the community, is to provide a comprehensive, caring education experience which

- Nurtures the unique talents of each individual
- Creates a fulfilled, socially responsible, life-long learner
- Develops confidence and capabilities to face the challenges of a rapidly changing world
- Promotes a culture of respect which values diversity

As partners, we will provide sufficient resources and a talented, committed staff that creates a safe environment where all individuals flourish.

Belief Statement

- We believe in the worth and dignity of each person.
- We believe that all students are entitled to the opportunity to maximize their talents and abilities.
- We believe that students thrive in a learning environment that facilitates self-discovery, exploration, and intellectual risk-taking.
- We believe that a quality education is a life-long process that fosters academic and cultural understanding.
- We believe that an effective education is a shared responsibility by all persons, groups, and organizations within our community.
- We believe that we have the obligation to nurture a culture of respect that honors the uniqueness of the individual and fosters responsibility toward the community and the environment.
- We believe that an effective educational system anticipates, plans and acts in response to a changing world.

Redlands Community Hospital
Redlands, California

Mission Statement

Our mission is to promote an environment where members of our community can receive high quality care and service so they can maintain and be restored to good health.

We will accomplish our mission by interacting with the following groups:

Our Patients
Our patients are not just customers, but are fellow humans in need. From their first encounter, we will treat our patients with dignity and compassion, comfort their family and friends, and endeavor to make their stay with us as rewarding as possible. We will provide whatever services we can, in and outside of the hospital, to maintain and restore the health of those who come to us for care.

Our Physicians
We shall strive to anticipate and meet the needs of the physicians who have chosen to affiliate with our hospital. Together with us, they shall govern themselves and continue to maintain and assure a superior standard of conduct and patient care.

Our Employees
Our employees are health professionals, trained not just to accomplish their jobs, but to realize that the purpose of every job is to benefit the patient.

Our Associates
Those who have had the faith in us to invest in our future and those with whom we do business deserve a return of that trust. We shall conduct our business efficiently for that purpose.

Our Community
We are an integral part of our community. Therefore, we will listen to our community and its leaders to help us assess the community's health needs and we will work with them to develop a plan to address those needs to the best of our abilities and resources.

Our Vision

Our vision is to be recognized for the quality of service we provide and our attention to patient care.

We want to remain a not-for-profit, full-service community hospital and to continue to be the major health care provider in our primary area of East San Bernardino Valley as well as the hospital of choice for our medical staff. We recognize the importance of remaining a financially strong organization and will take the necessary actions to ensure that we can fulfill this vision.

Our Values

We Are Committed to Serving Our Community.
Our services will make a difference in the quality of life in the communities we serve. It is our responsibility to assess the needs of our patients, physicians, employees, and others, and, to the best of our ability and resources, respond to those needs.

Our Community Deserves the Best We Can Offer.
We will provide efficient caring services to our patients and others in a courteous and professional way. We will strive to provide high quality, cost-efficient health care. We will continue to develop new services and eliminate obstacles to demonstrate our commitment of being responsive to the needs of our community.

Our Organization Will Be a Good Place to Work.
As an organization, we value the participation of each employee, physician, volunteer, and Board member. We will encourage suggestions, listen attentively, and follow through. Recognizing the importance of everyone who works here, we expect to treat one another, and to be treated, with respect and a sense of the importance of team work. Our greatest asset is the people who are committed to our organization.

Our Organization Will Be Financially Strong.
We will be a financially strong and creative organization with the people, facilities, and finances to provide our best service. We will create and maintain a financial environment that will support and encourage our values.

Northfield Retirement Community
Northfield, Minnesota

Vision
Northfield Retirement Community will be the best faith-based provider of compassionate, quality, services to the aging in the Cannon Valley. We will educate employees, families, and the communities we serve about the blessings of aging.

Mission
Northfield Retirement Community is a Christian church related not-for-profit organization dedicated to the development of a continuum of caring, living environments and outreach services, as works of love and mercy, primarily for older persons, to enable individuals to realize their maximum physical, spiritual, psychological and social potential.

Values
Because we believe our care-receivers and caregivers are people of significant worth, we will:

1. provide services without regard to religious preference, national origin, race, color, gender or disability;
2. uphold the right of residents to live with honor and dignity;
3. provide loving care to all residents with emphasis on service with excellence;
4. advocate on behalf of the people we serve within and beyond the campus of the Northfield Retirement Community; that will strengthen our capacity to meet the needs of the people we serve;
5. strive for the highest professional standards to guide our staff members in their daily tasks; foster a climate of opportunity to maximize their growth potential and recognize and accord them the respect due compassionate caregivers;
6. support volunteers and friends as important resources in the continuum of care; and embrace them as an integral piece of our caring and support ministry; and
7. be responsible financial stewards.

VA Iowa City Health Care System
Iowa City, Iowa

Mission – Vision – Values

- **Mission**

Dedicated to meeting the healthcare needs of veterans through quality patient care, education, and research.

- **Vision**

Recognized as:

- The provider of choice for veterans throughout our service area.
- A leader in the delivery of quality healthcare.
- A healthcare system dedicated to providing accessible healthcare.
- An employer of choice committed to employee growth and development.

- **Values**

- Trust
- Respect
- Excellence
- Commitment
- Compassion

Appendix C

Roles & Responsibilities of Board Officers

Board Chair

- Is a member in good standing of the Board of Directors
- Serves as Chair of the Executive Committee
- Serves as official signatory for corporate business, when required
- Presides over all board meetings, the annual meeting, and meetings of the Executive Committee
- Keeps the board focused on the organization's mission, vision, values and productive decision-making
- Encourages a positive board environment and respectful collaboration among all board members
- Insures that bylaws and policies governing the board are followed
- Respectfully corrects board members who are not fulfilling their commitment to the board
- Calls special meetings as needed
- Appoints all committee chairs in cooperation with the board
- Serves as an ex-officio member of all board committees
- Works with the Nominating Committee in recruiting new board members
- Oversees the process of leadership development within the board
- Oversees all fundraising efforts of the board
- Directs the board in strategic planning, in cooperation with the CEO
- Maintains a positive working relationship with the CEO
- Serves as the primary contact between the board and the CEO
- Works with the CEO to develop all board meeting agendas
- Works cooperatively with the CEO to address any areas of concern to the board
- Serves as official spokesperson for the board, as needed
- Works cooperatively with the CEO to develop and conduct new board member orientation
- Directs the search for a new CEO in cooperation with the Executive Committee and the board, as needed

- Directs the annual evaluation of the organization's success in achieving its mission and goals
- Directs the formal, annual evaluation of the CEO in cooperation with the Executive Committee and the board
- Directs the annual evaluation of the board

Vice Chair of the Board

- Is a member in good standing of the Board of Directors
- Serves on the Executive Committee
- Stays well-versed in the role and duties of the Chair
- Assumes the duties of the Chair in the Chair's absence
- Assists the Chair as needed
- Takes an active role in helping the Chair develop board leadership
- Serves as Chair of at least one standing committee

Secretary

- Is a member in good standing of the Board of Directors
- Serves on the Executive Committee
- Assumes the duties of the Chair in the absence of both the Chair and Vice Chair
- Is responsible for recording, storing and distributing all official meeting records and minutes
- Maintains a working knowledge of appropriate handling and storage of legal and organizational documents
- Keeps an accurate and updated roster of all members of the Board of Directors, including all necessary contact information, length of service, and remaining term in office

Treasurer

- Is a member in good standing of the Board of Directors
- Serves on the Executive Committee
- Assumes the duties of the Chair in the absence of the Chair, Vice Chair and Secretary

- Has an advanced knowledge of finance and accounting practices
- Serves on the Finance Committee
- Is responsible for obtaining, storing and distributing all financial information regarding the organization to the Finance Committee
- Is responsible for distributing financial documentation and regularly reporting to the Board of Directors regarding the financial status of the organization, in cooperation with the Finance Committee
- Makes recommendations to the board regarding the financial impact of decisions and policies being considered
- Advises the board in their review of financial policies
- Insures that fiscal policies set by the board are followed
- Maintains a good working relationship with the CFO and any outside financial consultants
- Serves as consultant with the CEO and assists with preparing the annual budget
- Evaluates the annual audit and assists in interpreting it

Appendix D

Fostering Dynamic Boards

Board Member Rights and Responsibilities

You have the right:

to an agenda

to know the purpose of the meeting before it starts

to your views and opinions

to be listened to when it's your turn

to disagree

to expect adherence to accepted rules of order

to ask for clarification when you need it

to be treated with dignity and respect

to expect that time will be used productively

You have the responsibility:

to be prepared

to be open to other viewpoints and opinions

to effectively listen to all sides of the issue

to work for mutual agreement

to adhere to accepted rules of order

to clearly communicate your ideas

to use diplomacy even when you disagree

to help keep the meeting focused on results

Appendix E - Example 1

Jurisdiction Agreement

Title: Executive Committee

Reports to: Board of Directors

Membership: Board Chair, Board Vice Chair, Board Secretary, Board Treasurer, Organization CEO

Purpose: To exercise interim power and authority of the board, when it is not practical or expeditious for the full board to meet; review the performance of the CEO and make recommendations to the full board; and serve in any administrative capacity, as requested by the board.

Act and Don't Report: The following decision areas allow for TOTAL jurisdiction. Appropriate action is expected to be taken without any reporting to the Board of Directors:

- Scheduling meetings as needed
- Assign tasks to committee members
- Request information from the CEO, necessary for committee operation

Act and Report: The following decision areas allow for TOTAL jurisdiction, providing report of such action is made to the Board of Directors in a timely manner:

- Exercise power and authority of the board when important matters require expeditious board action and it is not practical for the full board to meet

Report and Act: The following decision require approval of the Board of Directors PRIOR to any action being taken:

- Conduct annual CEO performance review, based on board and CEO-approved criteria
- Coordinate the process of hiring a new CEO when required

Appendix E – Example 2

Jurisdiction Agreement

Position Title: Administrator

Reports to: Board of Directors

Directly Supervises: Department managers and executive office staff

Purpose: To direct the day-to-day operation of the organization in a way that is in compliance with the mission, vision and values, strategic plan, board directives and policies, and applicable state, federal and local laws.

Act and Don't Report: The following decision areas allow for TOTAL jurisdiction. Appropriate action is expected to be taken without any reporting to the Board of Directors:

- Hiring, evaluating and firing of management personnel
- Scheduling of personal paid time off (P.T.O.)
- Transfer agreements with other institutions
- Release of funds to pay normal budgeted expenditures
- Disciplinary procedures as per employee handbook
- Salary adjustments under $500 to reflect change in employment or anniversary increases
- Obtaining Administrative clock hours of a minimum 30 hours per year for licensure

Act and Report: The following decision areas allow for TOTAL jurisdiction, providing report of such action is made to the Board of Directors in a timely manner:

- Maintaining institutional insurance programs
- Development and implementation of realistic wage scales and benefits
- Maintaining adequate accounting methods and procedures for monthly and yearly reports
- Employee advancements and personal growth and development opportunities
- Awarding of service contracts and agreements
- Job description development and implementation

199

Act and Report: (continued)

- Implementation of operating policies and procedures
- Emergency repairs and/or replacement of equipment
- Staffing of hours for each department
- Salary adjustments over $500 to reflect change in employment status

Report and Act: The following decision require approval of the Board of Directors PRIOR to any action being taken:

- Establishment of yearly operating budget
- Budget revisions, if necessary
- Investment strategies

Appendix F

Fostering Dynamic Boards

Association Steering Committee Meeting Agenda

Date _____ Start Time _____ Duration _____ Location_____

Meeting Facilitator _____ Phone # _____

Item	Person	Purpose*	Time
Need for set meeting times	JP	Decide	10m
Need for predictable meeting format	JP	Develop	30m
Information on taping and note taking	JR	Clarify	10m
Status report on administration meeting	NJ	Inform	15m
Discuss and finalize first recommendation	CJ	Clarify & Decide	1h 10m
Break			10m
Determine next recommendation	JP	Decide	10m
Other business	JP	Inform	15m
Set next agenda	JP	Decide	15m

* Debate - Decide - Develop - Clarify - Create - Inform

Appendix G

Peer Evaluation Form

Person You Are Evaluating _____ Date_____

Please answer the following questions by circling your response:

     1 = NEVER   2 = SELDOM   3 = SOMETIMES   4 = OFTEN   5 = ALWAYS

1.	Is on time for meetings	1	2	3	4	5
2.	Is prepared for meetings	1	2	3	4	5
3.	Is open to the opinions of others	1	2	3	4	5
4.	Is a good listener	1	2	3	4	5
5.	Is clear and understandable when speaking	1	2	3	4	5
6.	Is concise when speaking	1	2	3	4	5
7.	Is respectful of others	1	2	3	4	5
8.	Actively contributes to the group process	1	2	3	4	5
9.	Helps keep the group on track	1	2	3	4	5
10.	Demonstrates a positive attitude	1	2	3	4	5
11.	Maintains confidentiality outside of the group	1	2	3	4	5
12.	Focuses on solutions rather than problems	1	2	3	4	5

Next Person You Are Evaluating _____

Please answer the following questions by circling your response:

     1 = NEVER   2 = SELDOM   3 = SOMETIMES   4 = OFTEN   5 = ALWAYS

1.	Is on time for meetings	1	2	3	4	5
2.	Is prepared for meetings	1	2	3	4	5
3.	Is open to the opinions of others	1	2	3	4	5
4.	Is a good listener	1	2	3	4	5
5.	Is clear and understandable when speaking	1	2	3	4	5
6.	Is concise when speaking	1	2	3	4	5
7.	Is respectful of others	1	2	3	4	5
8.	Actively contributes to the group process	1	2	3	4	5
9.	Helps keep the group on track	1	2	3	4	5
10.	Demonstrates a positive attitude	1	2	3	4	5
11.	Maintains confidentiality outside of the group	1	2	3	4	5
12.	Focuses on solutions rather than problems	1	2	3	4	5

Appendix H

Fostering Dynamic Boards

Guidelines for CEO Evaluation

Objective Evaluation:

70% of the evaluation should be an Objective assessment of the achievement of organizational goals as measured by pre-defined gauges.

- Gauges should be based on critical performance indicators of organizational success.

- Gauges should be measurable and feasible -- where data can be obtained in a reliable, timely and cost-effective way.

- Gauges used in the evaluation of the CEO should only relate to areas where the CEO has control over the results. Example: "The CEO maintains a level of customer satisfaction that is equal to or greater than industry standards."

- The evaluation of the CEO should be the responsibility of the entire board, with the Board Chair and Executive Committee leading the process

- Gauges should be agreed upon by the board and the CEO prior to any evaluation period. The CEO should provide input for the creation of gauges and how they will be measured.

- Measurement process and evaluation criteria should also be agreed upon by the board and the CEO prior to any evaluation period.

- The evaluation's effect on compensation should be agreed upon by the board and the CEO prior to any evaluation period.

- The evaluation process should also include a CEO self-evaluation, based on the established outcomes.

- In any gauge area, the CEO may file an Exception Report for any unavoidable performance deviation. This will be taken into account during the evaluation process.

Subjective Evaluation:

30% of the evaluation should be a Subjective assessment of the CEO's leadership ability, based on pre-determined criteria defined by a consensus of the board. Example: "The CEO is a clear communicator." The input to make this assessment can be derived through the following methods:

- Board member assessments and observations

- Input from senior staff

- Input from other reliable resources (community leaders, professional organizations, etc.)

The Executive Committee, under the direction of the Board Chair, then takes all the information; reviews it, compiles it and makes recommendations to the entire board for any final discussion and approval, prior to conducting the actual review with the CEO.

Appendix I

Fostering Dynamic Boards

Ten Symptoms of Dysfunctional Boards Rating Form

Mild .... Severe

	Mild .... Severe
Foggy Focus	1 2 3 4 5
Dollar $ign Delusion	1 2 3 4 5
Bigger is Better Fixation	1 2 3 4 5
Dysfunctional Diversity	1 2 3 4 5
Turnstile Leadership	1 2 3 4 5
Altruistic Self-interest	1 2 3 4 5
Jurisdictional Jungle	1 2 3 4 5
Misguided Meetings	1 2 3 4 5
Decision Paralysis	1 2 3 4 5
Minutia Mania	1 2 3 4 5

A score of 3 or above on any symptom means your board has work to do.